1988

for looking at

all animals

ILLUSTRATED LIBRARY OF COOKING

VOLUME 2 Bir-Bre

In this volume: *the most
exciting poultry recipes*
FAMILY CIRCLE *has
developed through the years
—chicken, turkey, duck,
goose and game hen . . .
and for those who yen to
bake their own breads, a huge
collection of yeast breads
and quick breads, doughnuts
and fritters, waffles and
pancakes . . . PLUS a full
section on jazzing up
breakfasts.*

ROCKVILLE HOUSE PUBLISHERS, INC.
ROCKVILLE CENTRE, NEW YORK 11570

Family Circle®

Illustrated Library of

COOKING

YOUR READY REFERENCE FOR A LIFETIME OF GOOD EATING

Off-beat but beautiful and nutritionally sound, this breakfast combo: crisp crescents of pear and butter-smooth chunks of banana teamed with ocean-sweet Alaska king crab. It's a favorite on the West Coast.

Table of Contents

BIRDS OF A FEATHER

BIRDS OF A FEATHER:
SOME POULTRY SHOPPING TIPS,
HOW TO STUFF AND TRUSS POULTRY,
WINES TO SERVE WITH POULTRY,
CHICKEN, TURKEY, DUCKLING,
GOOSE, ROCK CORNISH GAME HENS

A bird in your shopping cart means the start of a good meal at a good price. If you compare what each dollar of your meat budget will buy, you will find that economically poultry is hard to beat. For variety of choice, ways to cook, nutrition, and popularity, it rates at the top, too. It is also easily available in any season. One reason for this is the fact that today poultry-raising—and that includes turkey, duckling, game hen and goose, as well as chicken—is big business.

Our modern birds are a pampered lot. They are scientifically bred and fed specially blended foods to make them plump and juicy. Efficient processing and speedy refrigerated transportation guarantee carefully controlled quality food. The fowls you buy are mass-produced for their meat; broiler-fryer chickens, for example, differ from egg-producing chickens the way beef cattle differ from dairy cows. In days past, it took months to raise a bird for market; now it takes just weeks and the savings show up

in the price at your supermarket. No wonder we eat about five times as much poultry today as we did twenty years ago.

SOME POULTRY SHOPPING TIPS

For Top Quality: Buy by brand name, government inspection mark and grade, or the stamp of your favorite dependable supermarket.

About Inspection: By federal law, all ready-to-cook fresh poultry from another state, as well as the frozen and canned poultry, is inspected for cleanliness and marked with a circle stamp.

135

INSPECTION MARK

USDA
A
GRADE

GRADE MARK

INSPECTED
FOR WHOLESOMENESS
BY
U.S.
DEPARTMENT OF
AGRICULTURE
P-00

Basic Broiled Chicken, shown here with a teaspoon of tarragon added to the basting butter for flavor.

In addition, most states have some inspection laws of their own that apply within the state. Some plants use their own grade or quality rating.

About Grading: Though government grading is not mandatory, a great many of the birds coming to market do bear the shield-shaped grade stamp. Top grade is USDA Grade A (young and tender, well-fleshed fowl with only slight bruises or discolorations), second best is USDA Grade B (leaner birds with moderate cuts or tears) and finally, USDA Grade C, which is rarely ever seen in retail markets. Often the inspection circle and grade shield appear together on a tag attached to the bird.

ABOUT BUYING CHICKEN:

Types Available: *Broiler-Fryer:* Meaty, tender all-purpose chicken that can be cooked by any method. About 9 weeks old, broiler-fryers weigh 1½ to 3½ pounds.

Roaster: Slightly larger and older than broiler-fryers, roasters weigh 3½ to 5 pounds and are best when roasted.

Stewing Chicken or Bro-Hen: A plump meaty bird, usually a year old or a little older that weighs 4½ to 6 pounds. These birds are tougher than broiler-fryers or roasters and are thus best when stewed or made into soup.

Capon: Fleshy, tender, desexed rooster with a high proportion of white meat and a fine flavor. Capons weigh 4 to 7 pounds and are excellent when roasted, steamed or stewed.

Chicken in Parts: In most markets today, it is possible to buy only that part of the chicken you want—all breasts, for example, all drumsticks, all wings, thighs or backs.

Other Forms of Chicken: Besides the many kinds of fresh chicken available, you can also buy chicken frozen or canned—handy to have on hand as insurance against drop-in guests.

136

How Much To Buy: Here are rules to follow in deciding how much chicken to buy, although you may want to increase these portions for big eaters in the family:

Chicken for Frying: Allow ¾ to 1 pound per serving.

Chicken for Roasting: Allow ¾ to 1 pound per serving.

Chicken for Broiling or Barbecuing: Allow ½ chicken or 1 pound per serving.

Chicken for Stewing: Allow ½ to 1 pound per serving.

Count on about 1 cup of cut-up cooked meat from each 1 pound of uncooked stewing chicken. You will need more when making a salad, or slicing for sandwiches and cold cuts, than when fixing a casserole or creamed dish.

ABOUT BUYING TURKEY

Types Available: (Note: The majority of turkeys now being marketed are frozen.)

Fryer-Roasters: Small meaty turkeys weighing in at from 4 to 9 pounds:

Roasters: These range in size from about 10 to 30 pounds for a Banquet Tom. The advantage of substituting two small birds for one giant is that you double the number of drumsticks, thighs, wings and breasts. The disadvantage is that small birds may not look quite so festive on the groaning board.

Boneless Turkey Roasts: Plump roasts weighing from 2 to 8 pounds.

Turkey Parts: Turkey drumsticks, wings, thighs and sometimes breasts are beginning to be marketed the way chicken parts are. The legs and wings, particularly, offer good eating at relatively low cost.

Frozen Pre-Stuffed Turkeys: Available in a broad range of sizes from small "junior" turkeys to near 20 pounders. Most popular are those in the 8 to 12 pound class.

Frozen Self-Basting Turkeys: Injected with butter before being frozen, these turkeys do actually baste themselves as they cook, taking a lot of the drudge out of the job. They are available in a wide range of sizes.

Frozen Boneless Turkey Rolls: These are available raw, fully cooked or smoked, as all dark or all white meat or combinations of the two. Weights range from 3 to 10 pounds.

Frozen Turkey Steaks: Turkey minute steaks, available plain and breaded.

Smoked Turkey: A gourmet item, ready to slice and eat.

How Much to Buy: When buying turkeys under 12 pounds, allow ¾ to 1 pound per serving; when buying birds weighing more than 12 pounds, allow ½ to ¾ pound per serving (there is proportionately more meat on the big birds).

ABOUT BUYING DUCKLING:

Types Available: Most of the ducklings coming to market today are Long Island Ducklings—succulent and meltingly tender. They are individually packed and quick-frozen although some areas sell fresh ice-chilled ducklings. Weights range from 4 to 6 pounds. Also beginning to appear in supermarkets are duckling parts, quick frozen and accompanied by full cooking instructions.

Everyone's Thanksgiving favorite, a whopping-big turkey, broad-breasted and roasted to a golden turn underneath lavish bastings of drippings.

How Much To Buy: Allow about ¼ duckling per person. Each bird cuts neatly into quarters with poultry shears. Directions for carving whole ducklings are included in the recipe section.

ABOUT BUYING GOOSE:

Types Available: These birds are less frequently seen in supermarkets than chickens, turkeys or ducklings, but quick-frozen ones are beginning to appear in big city areas with some regularity. And, of course, they can be ordered. They are tender and rich and weigh anywhere from 5 to 15 pounds. Those weighing 10 to 12 pounds are best for stuffing and roasting.

How Much To Buy: Allow ¾ to 1 pound ready-to-cook goose per person.

ABOUT BUYING ROCK CORNISH GAME HEN:

Types Available: This is a specially bred, very small chicken weighing 1½ pounds or less; it is available frozen in supermarkets across the country.

How Much To Buy: Allow 1 game hen per person.

HOW TO STORE AND FREEZE POULTRY

Fresh Poultry: Poultry is perishable—the minute you get home from the supermarket, unwrap the bird and remove giblets (heart, gizzard, liver) which come separately wrapped in a little package (often it is tucked into the body cavity). Rewrap bird *loosely* in wax paper, foil or transparent wrap and place it in the meat compartment or on the coldest shelf of your refrigerator. It will keep for one to two days. Store giblets separately and cook as soon as possible, within 24 hours.

If you wish to freeze the bird, unwrap it (again, do this as soon as you get home), discard all market wrappings and rinse bird in cold running water. Pat dry, then wrap the clean bird tightly in transparent wrap, foil or freezer paper and place in your freezer. It will keep two or three months. Never freeze an uncooked *stuffed* bird; the stuffing will spoil.

Frozen Poultry: Hard-frozen poultry may go right from your shopping cart into your freezer without being rewrapped. *But do not allow it to thaw at all in route.* If for any reason the bird has thawed, cook it promptly and *then* freeze it. Never refreeze the thawed raw bird.

137

Should frozen poultry be thawed before cooking? Depends on how it's to be cooked. If you're making stew, the bird can go into the kettle frozen. But for frying, broiling, barbecuing or roasting, it's better to thaw the fowl first, because it cooks more evenly that way. The best way to defrost frozen poultry is to take it from the freezer a day or two ahead and put it into the refrigerator. Don't unwrap it, because the skin tends to dry and toughen when exposed to air. You can hasten thawing by placing the frozen bird, still in its freezer wrap, under *cold* running water. Once it is thawed, don't lose time in cooking it.

Cooked Poultry: A bird that has been cooked ahead for a meal to be eaten during the next day or two can be kept, covered, in a cold part of the refrigerator. A leftover bird, similarly, can be placed in a covered container immediately after the meal and kept in the refrigerator for two or three days. Refrigerate broth or gravy in separate covered containers. Remove any stuffing from stuffed birds and store that separately too. Use within a couple of days.

Cooked poultry can go into your freezer cooled and tightly wrapped and can be kept for a month before serving. In freezing a leftover roasted bird, you should transfer it from refrigerator to freezer within 24 hours after roasting. It will save space to cut away meat from the bones first (you will have no future use for the carcass) and freeze only the meat. Wrap in transparent wrap, freezer paper or aluminum foil, label with amount (cup measure or number of slices) and date. Use within one month.

HOW TO STUFF AND TRUSS POULTRY

First rinse bird completely clean with cold running water inside and out. Pat dry. Rub the cavity lightly with salt.

1 Spoon stuffing lightly into neck (do not pack, for stuffing expands when cooking). Pull neck skin over the opening and fasten to back with a skewer or toothpick.

2 Stuff body cavity lightly. Close the opening by running skewers or toothpicks through the skin from one side of the opening to the other; then lace securely with string in a crisscross fashion. Or, you can sew the opening closed with a large needle and thread.

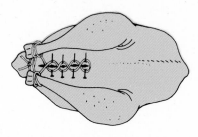

3 Loop the same string around the drumstick ends and tie them together, then fasten them to the tailpiece.

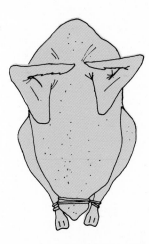

4 Fold wings up and over the back; this will help brace the bird in the roasting pan. Brush lightly with melted butter or margarine and place, breast up, in a roasting pan.

Or, if barbecuing on a spit:

4 Press wings close to breast and run a string around under the bird to completely encircle it, securing the wings snugly against the breast. The bird should be tied so that it makes a compact bundle.

WINES TO SERVE WITH POULTRY

Wine adds a festive touch to any poultry meal, and half the fun is knowing that the wine you choose is the right wine for the meal you are serving. A few good rules are:

- Dishes full of taste seem to demand *full, rich wines,* such as those from the Rhône or Burgundy regions of France. These wines reach their peak when they are 6 years or older.
- Dishes delicate in flavor call for *light wines,* usually white, rosé, or young red wines such as Beaujolais. White wines taste best when they are about 2 years old. Light red wines should be about 4 years old, except Beaujolais, which should be drunk when they are as young as possible.

The best way to go about selecting wine is to have a list of light wines—white or red—and a list of full wines, mostly red. So here they are, country by country:

FULL WINES

For roast goose and duck, barbecued birds, hearty stews, full-flavored casseroles and baked dishes, and fowl with zesty sauces or spicy glazes:

California Reds
Zinfandel
Pinot Noir
Cabernet Sauvignon

Italian Reds
Chianti
Barolo

French Reds
Bordeaux (such as St.-Emilion or Pomerol)
Burgundy (such as Nuits-St.-Georges, Vosne-Romanée, Clos de Vougeot, Chambolle-Musigny, Morey-St.-Denis, Gevrey-Chambertin, Fixin)
Rhône (such as Châteauneuf-du-Pape or Hermitage)

French Whites
Rhône (Hermitage Blanc)

Alsatian Whites
Sylvaner, Traminer, Gewürztraminer

LIGHT WINES

For fried chicken, broiled chicken or turkey, simple chicken, turkey or Rock Cornish Game

Hen roasts, lightly flavored stews and pies, and such cold dishes as salads and sandwiches:

California Whites
Mountain White
Pinot Blanc
Gray Riesling
Pinot Chardonnay
Johannisberger Riesling

California Reds
Mountain Red

German Whites
Liebfraumilch
Steinwein
Moselblümchen
Mosel (one from Graach or Bernkastel)
Rheinpfalz (one from Ruppertsberg or Forst)
Rheinhessen (one from Oppenheim or Nierstein)
Rheingau (one from Eltville or Erbach)

Italian Whites
Verdicchio
Orvieto
Soave

Italian Reds
Bardolino
Valpolicella

French Whites
Loire (such as Pouilly-Fumé or Muscadet)
Alsace (such as Pinot Gris or Riesling)
Bordeaux (such as Graves)
Burgundy (such as Pouilly-Fuissé or Meursault) (*Note:* a white Burgundy such as Chablis, while too dry for most chicken or turkey, is excellent with pâtés, chicken liver dishes, and dishes or stuffings that include shellfish.)

French Reds
Rhône (such as Côtes du Rhône)
Burgundy (such as Beaujolais, Côtes de Beaune-Villages, Chassagne-Montrachet, Volnay, Pommard, Santenay, Beaune, Monthélie)
Bordeaux (such as Graves, Médoc, Haut-Médoc)

PINK WINES

Many people prefer pink wines to accompany Oriental or lightly-flavored chicken dishes. Good choices are rosés from Anjou or Portugal.

SHERRY

With appetizers and soups, a dry chilled sherry is delicious, especially one called Fino or Manzanilla. Sherry is also the drink to serve when your poultry dish has sherry in the sauce.

CHAMPAGNE

The all-purpose wine champagne can accompany any poultry dish. When served with food, a "sec" (dry) usually tastes better than one labeled "brut," which is very very dry.

CHICKEN

Double-Treat Roast Chicken

Let your guests choose their favorite dressing and share the delicious gravy.
Roast at 375° for 1¼ hours. Makes 8 servings

    2 broiler-fryers (about 2½ pounds each)
    3 cups water
      Handful of celery leaves
    2 onion slices
    ½ teaspoon salt
      Dash of pepper
    4 tablespoons (½ stick) butter or margarine,
      melted
      Fruited Giblet Dressing (recipe follows)
      Jardiniere Dressing (recipe follows)
    2 teaspoons aromatic bitters
      Chicken Gravy (recipe follows)

1 Remove chicken giblets from chickens and return chicken and livers to refrigerator. Combine giblets, water, celery leaves, onion slices, salt and pepper in medium-size saucepan. Heat to boiling; reduce heat and simmer 50 minutes. Add chicken livers and cook 10 minutes longer, or until giblets are tender. Trim and finely chop giblets. Strain and reserve broth.
2 Stuff one chicken with *Fruited Giblet Dressing* and one chicken with *Jardiniere Dressing*. Place in shallow roasting pan. Brush chickens with part of melted butter or margarine.
3 Roast in moderate oven (375°), basting several times with pan drippings, 1 hour. Stir bitters into remaining melted butter. Brush over chickens. Roast 15 minutes longer, or until chickens are golden. Place on heated serving platter and keep warm while making *Chicken Gravy*. Garnish platter with bundles of cooked carrots and green beans and parsley, if you wish.

140

Fruited Giblet Dressing

Makes 1½ cups or enough to stuff one 2½-pound chicken

    1 large apple, pared, cored and chopped
    2 tablespoons butter or margarine
      Chopped giblets
    1½ cup soft bread crumbs (3 slices)
    3 tablespoons giblet broth
    ½ teaspoon salt
    ¼ teaspoon ground allspice
      Dash of pepper

Sauté apple until soft in butter or margarine in skillet. Stir in chopped giblets and cook 2 minutes. Stir in bread crumbs, broth, salt, allspice and pepper until well-blended.

Jardiniere Dressing

Makes 1½ cups or enough to stuff one 2½-pound chicken

    1 medium-size onion, chopped (½ cup)
    ½ cup finely chopped celery
    ½ cup finely chopped carrots
    2 tablespoons butter or margarine
    1 cup soft bread crumbs (2 slices)
    ½ teaspoon leaf savory, crumbled
    ½ teaspoon salt
      Dash of pepper

Sauté onion, celery and carrots until soft in butter or margarine in skillet. Stir in bread crumbs, savory, salt and pepper until well-blended.

Chicken Gravy

Makes about 2½ cups

Stir 4 tablespoons flour into pan drippings. Cook, stirring constantly, 3 minutes. Blend in remaining giblet broth. (You should have 2½ cups.) Cook, stirring constantly, until mixture thickens and bubbles 3 minutes.

Little Chicken Roasts

Everyone rates a half chicken with the best pineapple stuffing! And a mild sweet-sour sauce goes with it.
Roast at 375° for 1½ hours. Makes 6 servings

    3 broiler-fryers (about 1½ pounds each)
    ½ cup (1 stick) butter or margarine

Two chickens in one pot, in this case, casserole-roasted chickens on a bed of noodles and mushrooms.

BIRDS OF A FEATHER

1 can (about 9 ounces) crushed pineapple
3 cups soft bread crumbs (6 slices)
½ cup flaked coconut (from a 3½-ounce can)
½ cup chopped celery
½ teaspoon salt
¼ teaspoon poultry seasoning
2 tablespoons bottled steak sauce
Sweet-and-Sour Sauce (recipe follows)

1 Rince chickens inside and out with cold water; drain, then pat dry. Sprinkle inside with salt.
2 Melt butter or margarine in a small saucepan. Drain syrup from pineapple into a cup and set aside for making glaze in Step 6.
3 Combine pineapple with bread crumbs, coconut, and celery in a medium-size bowl; drizzle 4 tablespoons of the melted butter or margarine over; toss with a fork until crumbs are lightly coated. (Save remaining butter or margarine for Step 5.)
4 Stuff neck and body cavities of chickens lightly with pineapple-bread mixture. Smooth neck skin over stuffing and skewer to back; tie legs to tail with heavy white string. Place chickens in a roasting pan.
5 Stir salt and poultry seasoning into saved 4 tablespoons melted butter or margarine in saucepan; brush part over chickens.
6 Roast in moderate oven (375°), basting several times with butter mixture, 1 hour. Stir saved pineapple syrup and steak sauce into any remaining butter in saucepan; brush generously over chickens.
7 Continue roasting, basting once or twice more, 30 minutes longer, or until drumsticks move easily and meaty part of thigh feels soft.
8 Remove chickens to heated serving platter; keep warm while making *Sweet-and-Sour Sauce*.
9 When ready to serve, cut away strings from chickens. Garnish platter with water cress and preserved mixed fruits, if you wish. Pass sauce in a separate bowl to spoon over.

SWEET-AND-SOUR SAUCE—Blend 2 tablespoons cornstarch into drippings in roasting pan; stir in 1 cup water. Cook, stirring all the time, just until mixture thickens and boils 3 minutes. Stir in 2 tablespoons brown sugar and 1 tablespoon lemon juice. Strain into heated serving bowl. Makes about 1¼ cups.

142

Polynesian Chicken Platter

Mild curry-bacon sauce glazes the chickens to a sparkly gold. Rice stuffing has a double-nut seasoning.
Bake at 350° for 2 hours. Makes 6 to 8 servings

2 roasting chickens (about 4 pounds each)
Hilo Stuffing (recipe follows)

3 tablespoons butter or margarine, melted
Curry-fruit Glaze (recipe follows)

1 Rinse chickens inside and out with cold water; drain, then pat dry. Stuff neck and body cavities lightly with *Hilo Stuffing*. Smooth neck skin over stuffing and skewer to back; tie legs to tails with string.
2 Place chickens on a rack in a roasting pan; brush with melted butter or margarine.
3 Roast in moderate oven (350°) 1 hour.
4 Spoon part of the *Curry-Fruit Glaze* over each to make a thick coating. Continue roasting, basting two or three times with remaining glaze, 1 hour, or until drumsticks move easily and chickens are glazed.
5 Remove to a heated serving platter; cut away strings and remove skewers.

Hilo Stuffing

Macadamia nuts and coconut give this rice stuffing a gourmet flair.
Makes 4 cups, or enough to stuff 2 four-pound chickens

1 cup uncooked regular rice
4 tablespoons (½ stick) butter or margarine
1 medium-size onion, chopped (½ cup)
2 envelopes instant chicken broth
OR: 2 chicken bouillon cubes
2½ cups water
½ cup chopped macadamia nuts (from a 6-ounce jar)
½ cup flaked coconut (from a 3½-ounce can)

1 Sauté rice in butter or margarine, stirring often, just until golden in a large saucepan.
2 Stir in onion, chicken broth or bouillon cubes, and water; heat to boiling, crushing cubes, if using, with a spoon; cover. Simmer 20 minutes, or until rice is tender and liquid is absorbed.
3 Sprinkle with nuts and coconut; toss lightly to mix.

Curry-Fruit Glaze

Canned strained apples-and-apricots mellow the flavor of this exotic sauce.
Makes 1½ cups, or enough to glaze 2 four-pound chickens

4 slices bacon, diced
1 medium-size onion, chopped
2 tablespoons flour
1 tablespoon sugar
2 teaspoons curry powder
½ teaspoon salt
1 tablespoon bottled steak sauce

Little Chicken Roasts, filled with a pineapple and bread stuffing, served with Sweet-and-Sour Sauce.

1 cup water
2 tablespoons lemon juice
1 jar (4 ounces) baby-pack strained apples-and-apricots

1 Sauté bacon until crisp in a medium-size saucepan; remove and drain on paper toweling.
2 Stir onion into drippings in saucepan; sauté just until soft. Stir in flour, sugar, curry powder, and salt; heat until bubbly.
3 Stir in remaining ingredients and bacon. Simmer, stirring several times, 15 minutes, or until thick.

●

Casserole-Roasted Chicken
Bake at 325° for 1¼ hours. Makes 4 servings

 1 broiler-fryer (about 3 pounds)
1½ teaspoon salt
 ¼ teaspoon pepper
 16 small white onions, peeled
 12 small red, new potatoes
 3 tablespoons butter or margarine
 3 tablespoons vegetable oil
 ½ cup boiling water
 1 envelope instant chicken broth or 1 teaspoon granulated chicken bouillon
 1 teaspoon leaf basil, crumbled
 1 tablespoon chopped parsley

1 Sprinkle chicken cavities with ½ teaspoon of the salt and pepper. Peel onions. Scrub potatoes; pare a band around the center of each.
2 Melt butter or margarine with the vegetable oil in a large heavy flameproof casserole or Dutch oven. Add chicken; brown on all sides.
3 Combine boiling water and chicken broth in

Casserole-Roasted Chicken, scented with basil and roasted on a bed of white onions and new potatoes.

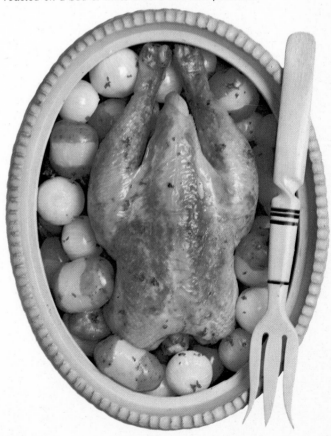

a 1-cup measure, stirring until dissolved; add to casserole with chicken.

4 Place onions and potatoes around chicken; sprinkle with basil and remaining 1 teaspoon salt; cover.

5 Bake in slow oven (325°), basting once or twice with juices, 1¼ hours, or until chicken and vegetables are tender. Sprinkle with parsley.

●

Country Roast Chicken

Bake at 350° for 1½ hours. Makes 8 servings

    2 broiler-fryers (about 3 pounds each)
    1 cup water
    ½ teaspoon salt
    1 package (8 ounces) corn bread stuffing mix
    1 medium-size onion, chopped (½ cup)
    ½ cup sliced celery
    ½ cup (1 stick) butter or margarine
    ¼ cup bacon drippings
        OR: ¼ cup (½ stick) butter or margarine,
        melted

1 Remove giblets and necks from chicken packages and place (except livers) with water and salt in a small saucepan; cover. Simmer 45 minutes. Add livers; cover; simmer 15 minutes longer; cool.

2 Remove giblets and necks from broth; reserve broth. Chop giblets and the meat from necks; place in a large bowl; stir in stuffing mix.

3 Simmer reserved broth until reduced to ½ cup; reserve.

4 Sauté onion and celery in the ½ cup butter or margarine for 5 minutes in a medium-size skillet. Add with reserved broth to stuffing mixture in bowl; toss until evenly moistened.

5 Stuff neck and body cavities lightly with stuffing. Skewer neck skin to back; close body cavity and tie legs to tail. Place chickens on rack in roasting pan. Brush with part of bacon drippings or butter or margarine.

6 Roast in moderate oven (350°) basting every 30 minutes with bacon drippings or butter or margarine, 1½ hours, or until tender.

7 To serve: Place on heated serving platter. Cut chickens into quarters with poultry shears.

● ● ●

HOW TO CARVE A CHICKEN

To carve roast chicken you need first of all a good, sharp, thin-bladed knife, and a sharp, long-tined fork. Keep your carving equipment in good condition, and do not use it for any purposes other than what it was intended for.

Before you begin to carve, be sure you remove from the chicken all the trussing equipment—skewers, toothpicks, cord, or thread.

Place the chicken breast-up on a serving platter or carving board large enough to make handling easy. You might have a separate plate nearby to hold drumsticks and wings out of the way as you remove them.

1 Place platter square in front of you, the chicken on its back with its legs toward your right. Grasping end of leg nearest you, bend it down toward platter while you cut through thigh joint to separate whole leg from body. Separate drumstick and thigh by cutting through joint.

2 Stick fork into breast near breastbone and cut off wing close to body. Slanting knife inward slightly may make it easier to hit the joint.

3 Slice white meat, starting at tip of breastbone and cutting down toward wing joint. Repeat with other side of chicken, turning platter if you wish.

144

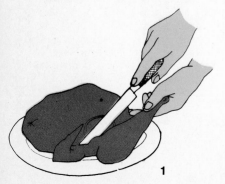

1

2

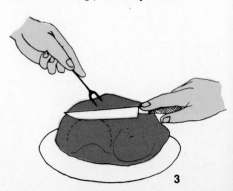

3

HOW TO CUT AND BONE A CHICKEN

1 Place chicken breast side up. Using a sharp knife, make lengthwise slit through skin and flesh from neck to cavity. Turn bird over and repeat cut.

2 Using poultry shears (**A**) or kitchen shears (**B**), cut right through bones (ribs). Cutting to one side of breastbone is easier than cutting through it.

3 Turn chicken over. Cut through bones, cutting to one side of the backbone. You may remove backbone. A small bird is cut this way for serving.

4 For quartering chicken, continue using shears. Cut across half the bird, following the natural division just below the rib cage and the breastbone.

5 Thigh may be left attached to leg for broiling; but for frying, bend leg joint. Cut through joint with a sharp knife, separating leg from the thigh.

6 To separate wing from the breast, bend joint. Cut through joint with a sharp knife. The chicken will now be in eight pieces and ready for frying.

7 If your recipe calls for skinned chicken breasts, use a sharp, small paring knife to start, then slip fingers between skin and flesh and peel skin.

8 To bone chicken breast, use a small paring knife. Cut meat away from rib bones with quick little strokes, feeling your way along with your fingers.

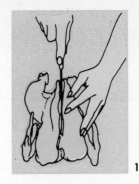

1

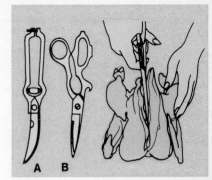

2

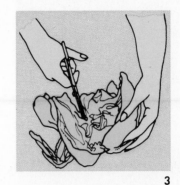

3

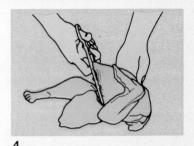

4

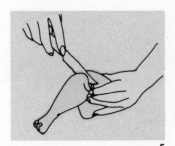

5

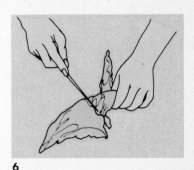

6

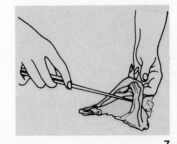

7

8

Baked Lemon Chicken
Bake at 375° for 1 hour. Makes 4 servings

  1 broiler-fryer (about 2½ pounds)
  ½ cup flour
1¼ teaspoons salt
  1 teaspoon leaf tarragon, crumbled
  ½ cup (1 stick) butter or margarine
  ⅓ cup lemon juice
  1 tablespoon instant minced onion
  1 clove of garlic, mashed
  ⅛ teaspoon pepper

1 Cut chicken into serving-size pieces.
2 Combine flour, 1 teaspoon of the salt, and tarragon in a plastic bag. Shake chicken in flour to coat; tap off excess.
3 Melt butter or margarine in a 13x9x2-inch

baking pan. Coat chicken on all sides in melted butter or margarine, then turn pieces skin-side up.

4 Bake in moderate oven (375°), brushing often with pan drippings, 30 minutes.

5 Meanwhile, make Lemon Baste: Mix lemon juice, instant minced onion, garlic, remaining ¼ teaspoon salt, and pepper in a small bowl. Brush chicken pieces with part of the Lemon Baste.

6 Bake, brushing occasionally with remaining Lemon Baste, 30 minutes longer, or until chicken is tender.

Spanish Chicken Bake

New Spanish-rice-seasoning mix gives this dish a mellow slow-cooked flavor.
Bake at 350° for 1 hour. Makes 8 servings

2 broiler-fryers (about 2½ pounds each), quartered
¼ cup flour
¼ cup vegetable oil
1½ cups uncooked regular rice
3 cups water
1 envelope Spanish-rice-seasoning mix
1 large green pepper, cut in 8 rings
1 cup sliced stuffed green olives

1 Shake chicken with flour in paper bag to coat well. Brown, a few pieces at a time, in vegetable oil in large frying pan; drain on paper toweling.

2 Place rice in a 10-cup shallow baking dish; arrange browned chicken on top.

3 Stir water into chicken drippings in frying pan; blend in Spanish-rice-seasoning mix; heat to boiling. Pour over chicken and rice; cover.

4 Bake in moderate oven (350°) 30 minutes; uncover and lay green-pepper rings and sliced olives on top. Cover and bake 30 minutes longer, or until chicken and rice are tender, and liquid is absorbed.

Chicken Imperial

Drumsticks, thighs, and breasts are stuffed with parsley-ham dressing, then breaded and baked in a creamy sauce.
Bake at 350° for 1 hour and 15 minutes. Makes 8 servings

2 cups soft bread crumbs (4 slices)
¾ cup finely diced cooked ham
½ cup chopped parsley
8 tablespoons (1 stick) hard butter or margarine, sliced thin

Chicken and zippily-flavored rice bake conveniently, harmoniously en casserole *in Spanish Chicken Bake.*

4 chicken breasts (about 12 ounces each)
4 chicken drumsticks with thighs
1 cup milk
1 cup fine dry bread crumbs
1 envelope (2 to a package) cream of mushroom soup mix
2 cups cold water
¼ cup chili sauce

1 Mix soft bread crumbs, ham, and parsley in a large bowl; cut in butter or margarine quickly with a pastry blender; chill while fixing chicken so butter doesn't melt.

2 Pull skin from chicken pieces; halve breasts, then cut out rib bones with scissors. Separate thighs and drumsticks at joints with a sharp knife. To make pockets for stuffing, pull each breast piece open on its thick side, and cut an opening along bone in each leg and thigh with a sharp-point knife.

3 Stuff about ¼ cup chilled stuffing into each half breast and 2 tablespoonfuls into each leg and thigh.

4 Place ½ cup of the milk in a pie plate and dry bread crumbs on a sheet of waxed paper. (Set remaining ½ cup milk aside for making sauce.) Roll stuffed chicken in milk, then in bread crumbs to coat well; chill while making sauce.

5 Combine mushroom soup mix and water in a small saucepan; cook, following label directions. Stir in remaining ½ cup milk and chili sauce; pour 1 cup into a shallow 12-cup baking dish.

6 Place chicken pieces, standing on edge if needed to fit, in sauce in dish; drizzle remaining sauce between pieces.

7 Bake in moderate oven (350°) 1 hour and 15 minutes, or until tender and richly golden. Garnish with parsley, if you wish.

Hostess note—If dinner is delayed, simply lower oven heat to very slow (250°) and fit a sheet of foil, tent fashion, over casserole. It will hold well about an hour.

●

Batter Crisp Chicken

Secret of this favorite is double cooking—baking first, then frying, covered with a puffy-golden jacket.

Bake at 350° for 1 hour. Makes 6 servings

2 broiler-fryers (about 2 pounds each), cut in serving-size pieces
2 teaspoons salt
1 teaspoon ground rosemary
½ cup water

One of the very best chicken recipes ever invented, crispily-crusted, richly golden Chicken Imperial.

Oven-Barbecued Chicken, superb on a summer's day with just-picked ears of sweet corn, dripping with butter, and crisp green salad. Dessert? Watermelon, of course.

Ginger Batter (recipe follows)
Shortening or vegetable oil for frying

148

1 Wash chicken pieces; pat dry. Place in a single layer in a large, shallow baking pan; sprinkle with salt and rosemary; add water; cover.
2 Bake in moderate oven (350°) 1 hour.
3 Remove chicken from pan; pull off skin and remove small rib bones, if you wish; drain chicken well on paper toweling.
4 While chicken cooks, prepare *Ginger Batter*.
5 Melt enough shortening or pour in enough vegetable oil to make a 2-inch depth in an electric deep-fat fryer or large saucepan; heat to 350°.
6 Dip chicken pieces, 2 or 3 at a time, into *Ginger Batter;* hold over bowl to let excess drip back.

7 Fry in hot fat 3 minutes, or until golden-brown. Lift out with a slotted spoon; drain well. Keep hot until all pieces are cooked.

Ginger Batter
Makes about 1½ cups

1¼ cups sifted all-purpose flour
1 teaspoon baking powder
1 teaspoon salt
½ teaspoon ground ginger
1 egg
1 cup milk
¼ cup vegetable oil

Sift flour, baking powder, salt, and ginger into a medium-size bowl. Add remaining ingredients all at once; beat with a rotary beater until smooth.

Oven-Barbecued Chicken

What a lazy-day way to turn out this picnic favorite! And it takes almost no watching.
Bake at 400° for 1 hour. Makes 4 servings

2 broiler-fryers (about 2 pounds each), quartered
1 large onion, cut into thick slices
⅔ cup catsup
⅓ cup vinegar
4 tablespoons (½ stick) butter or margarine
1 clove of garlic, minced
1 teaspoon leaf rosemary, crushed
1 teaspoon salt
¼ teaspoon dry mustard

1 Place chicken, skin-side down, in a single layer in a buttered shallow baking pan; top with onion slices.
2 Mix remaining ingredients in a small saucepan; heat to boiling; pour over chicken.
3 Bake in hot oven (400°) 30 minutes. Turn chicken, skin-side up; baste with sauce in pan. Continue baking, basting once or twice, 30 minutes longer, or until tender and richly glazed.

Old-Fashioned Chicken Pie

Bake at 400° for 30 minutes. Makes 8 servings

2 broiler-fryers (about 2½ pounds each)
Water
2 teaspoons salt
¼ teaspoon pepper
2 cups sliced carrots
1 package (10 ounces) frozen peas
¼ cup (½ stick) butter or margarine
6 tablespoons flour
1½ cups biscuit mix
½ cup dairy sour cream
1 egg
2 teaspoons sesame seeds

1 Place chickens in a large heavy kettle or Dutch oven; add 2 cups water, salt, pepper, and carrots. Heat to boiling; reduce heat; cover; simmer 45 minutes. Add peas; simmer 15 minutes longer, or until chicken is tender. Remove chicken to a large bowl to cool.
2 Skim fat from chicken broth-vegetable mixture; reserve 2 tablespoons fat. Melt butter or margarine with reserved chicken fat in a medium-size saucepan; stir in flour; cook, stirring constantly, just until bubbly. Stir in chicken broth-vegetable mixture; continue cooking and stirring until gravy thickens and bubbles 1 minute.
3 When chickens are cool enough to handle, pull off skin and slip meat from bones; cut meat into bite-size pieces; stir into gravy; pour into an 8-cup baking dish, 8x8x2.

4 Combine biscuit mix and sour cream in a small bowl; stir to form a stiff dough; turn out onto a lightly floured board; knead a few times; roll out dough to ¼-inch thickness; trim to make an 8½-inch square; cut into 8 strips, each about one inch wide.
5 Using 4 of the strips, make a lattice design on top of the chicken mixture, spacing evenly and attaching ends firmly to edges of the dish. Place remaining strips, one at a time, on edges of dish, pinching dough to make a stand-up rim; flute rim. (Or, roll out dough to a 9-inch square and place over chicken mixture; turn edges under, flush with rim; flute to make a stand-up rim. Cut slits near center to let steam escape.)
6 Combine egg with 1 tablespoon water in a cup; mix with a fork until well-blended; brush mixture over strips and rim; sprinkle with sesame seeds.
7 Bake in hot oven (400°) 30 minutes, or until chicken mixture is bubbly-hot, and crust is golden. Serve immediately.

Chicken in Walnut Sauce

Bake at 350° for 1¼ hours. Makes 8 servings

1 package (8 ounces) regular noodles
2 broiler-fryers (about 2 pounds each), cut in serving-size pieces
2 teaspoons salt
½ teaspoon leaf rosemary, crumbled
¼ teaspoon pepper
3 tablespoons butter or margarine
1 medium-size onion, chopped
4 tablespoons flour
1¾ cups milk

Luscious, lattice-topped Old-Fashioned Chicken Pie.

¼ cup dry white wine :
1 can (10½ ounces) condensed cream of
  chicken soup
1 can (4 ounces) walnuts, chopped
  Paprika

1 Cook noodles, following label directions;
drain well. Place in a refrigerator-to-oven baking
dish, 13x9x2.
2 Season chicken with 1½ teaspoons of the
salt, rosemary, and pepper. Brown, part at a
time, in butter or margarine in a large frying
pan; place in a single layer over noodles.
3 Stir onion into drippings in pan; sauté until
soft. Blend in flour; cook, stirring constantly,
until bubbly. Stir in milk and wine; continue
cooking and stirring until sauce thickens and
boils 1 minute. Stir in soup, walnuts, and remaining ½ teaspoon salt. Pour over mixture in
baking dish. Sprinkle with paprika. Cover; chill.
4 About 1 hour and 15 minutes before serving
time, place baking dish, covered, in moderate
oven (350°).
5 Bake 1 hour and 15 minutes, or until bubbly
and chicken is tender.

Hong Kong Chicken
Bake at 350° for 1½ hours. Makes 4 servings

1 broiler-fryer (about 3 pounds)
¼ cup water
¼ cup dry sherry
¼ cup soy sauce
¼ cup honey
2 teaspoons seasoned salt

1 Cut chicken into quarters; arrange in a single
layer in a 13x9x2-inch baking dish.
2 Mix water, sherry, soy sauce, honey, and
seasoned salt in a small bowl; pour over
chicken, turning to coat on all sides; cover.
Marinate chicken in refrigerator about 4 hours,
or overnight.
3 About 2 hours before serving time, remove
chicken from refrigerator; let stand at room
temperature 30 minutes, then drain; reserve
marinade. Arrange chicken, skin side up, on
rack in broiler pan, or in a shallow baking pan
with a rack. Brush generously with part of the
marinade.
4 Bake in moderate oven (350°), basting with
remaining marinade every 20 minutes, 1½
hours, or until chicken is tender and deep

golden brown. Place on heated serving platter;
serve with cooked frozen Chinese pea pods and
sliced water chestnuts, if you wish.

Chicken Stew
Big pieces of chicken bake in a zesty tomato
sauce. Croutons add a pleasing crunch.
Bake at 350° for 1 hour and 30 minutes. Makes
8 servings

6 slices bacon, cut in 1-inch pieces
2 broiler-fryers (about 2 pounds each), cut up
½ cup unsifted all-purpose flour
2 teaspoons salt
¼ teaspoon pepper
1 large onion, chopped
1 clove of garlic minced
1 can (3 or 4 ounces) whole mushrooms
2 cans (1 pound each) tomatoes
¼ cup chopped parsley
  Few drops liquid red pepper seasoning
  Golden Croutons (recipe follows)

1 Fry bacon until almost crisp in large frying
pan. Lift out with slotted spoon; drain on paper
toweling and set aside for Step 6. Leave drippings in pan.
2 Wash and dry chicken pieces well. Snip off
small rib bones with kitchen scissors, if you
wish. Shake chicken in mixture of flour, salt,
and pepper in paper bag to coat well. (Reserve
any leftover flour mixture for Step 4.)
3 Brown chicken, a few pieces at a time, in
bacon drippings; place in 12-cup shallow baking dish.
4 Sauté onion and garlic until soft in same
frying pan; stir in reserved flour mixture. Drain
liquid from mushrooms. (Save mushrooms for
Step 6.) Stir liquid, tomatoes, parsley, and red
pepper seasoning into frying pan; heat to boiling, stirring constantly.
5 Spoon over chicken in baking dish; cover.
(Casserole can be put together up to this point,
then chilled. Remove from refrigerator and let
stand at room temperature 30 minutes before
baking.)
6 Bake in moderate oven (350°) 1 hour and 20
minutes, or until chicken is tender. Uncover;
sprinkle with reserved bacon pieces and
mushrooms. Bake 10 minutes longer, or until
bacon is crisp.
7 Just before serving, sprinkle Golden Croutons over top; garnish with more chopped
parsley, if you wish.
   GOLDEN CROUTONS—Trim crusts from 2 slices
white bread; cut into ½-inch cubes. Spread in
single layer in shallow baking pan. Toast in
moderate oven (350°) 10 minutes, or until
golden. Makes 1 cup.

Golden Prize Party Chicken

Easiest way we know to cook chicken for a crowd.

Bake at 350° for 1 hour. Makes 8 servings, 2 pieces each

  2 broiler-fryers (about 2-2½ pounds each), cut in serving-size pieces
½ cup evaporated milk
  2 tablespoons prepared mustard
  2 teaspoons salt
½ teaspoon marjoram
  1 cup packaged corn-flake crumbs
¼ cup chopped parsley
  1 green onion, chopped

1 Cut away small bones from chicken breasts; remove all skin if you prefer chicken cooked without it. (Cook with backs and necks to make broth for another meal.)
2 Combine evaporated milk, prepared mustard, 1 teaspoon salt, and marjoram in pie plate; combine cornflake crumbs, parsley, green onion, and remaining 1 teaspoon salt in second pie plate.
3 Dip chicken pieces, 1 at a time, in evapo-rated-milk mixture; drain well, then roll in crumb mixture; arrange in single layer, pieces not touching, on cooky sheet lined with buttered aluminum foil.
4 Bake in moderate oven (350°) 1 hour, or until chicken is richly browned and tender when pierced with a fork.

●

Coq "Au Vin"

Long slow cooking gives this aristocrat the mellowest flavor. Its seasoning secrets: Apple cider and mixed vegetable juices.

Bake at 350° for 2 hours and 15 minutes. Makes 4 servings

  1 stewing chicken (about 4 pounds), cut in serving-size pieces
⅓ cup unsifted all-purpose flour
1½ teaspoons salt
  3 tablespoons butter or margarine
½ cup diced cooked ham
 12 small white onions, peeled
  1 can (12 ounces) mixed vegetable juices (1½ cups)
1½ cups apple cider
  1 can (3 or 4 ounces) mushroom caps
  1 clove garlic, minced
  6 peppercorns

151

An American favorite cooked with Oriental flair—Hong Kong Chicken wreathed with Chinese pea pods.

BIRDS OF A FEATHER

6 whole cloves
1 bay leaf

1 Wash chicken pieces; pat dry. Shake with flour and salt in a paper bag to coat well.
2 Brown pieces, a few at a time, in butter or margarine in a large frying pan; place in a 12-cup baking dish; sprinkle with ham and top with onions.
3 Stir vegetable juices, cider, mushrooms and liquid, and garlic into drippings in pan; heat to boiling, scraping brown bits from bottom of pan. Pour over chicken mixture.
4 Tie seasonings in a tiny cheesecloth bag; add to baking dish; cover.
5 Bake in moderate oven (350°) 2 hours and 15 minutes, or until chicken is very tender.
6 Uncover; remove spice bag and let chicken stand for 5 to 10 minutes, or until fat rises to top, then skim off. Garnish chicken with parsley, if you wish.

Chicken Sauté, Normandy Style
Makes 6 servings

2 broiler-fryers (about 1½ pounds each)
1 tablespoon vegetable oil
2 tablespoons butter or margarine
2 tablespoons applejack
1 medium-size onion, finely chopped (½ cup)
½ cup sliced celery
2 tablespoons chopped parsley
1 teaspoon salt
¾ teaspoon leaf thyme, crumbled
⅛ teaspoon pepper
1 cup apple cider
2 egg yolks
1 cup light cream or table cream

1 Cut chickens into serving-size pieces. Brown well on all sides in oil and butter or margarine in a large heavy kettle or Dutch oven; remove from heat.
2 Warm the applejack in a small saucepan until small bubbles appear around edge. (Do not boil.) Carefully ignite with a wooden match held at arm's length. Quickly pour over chicken, shaking gently until flames die. Remove chicken to a heated platter; keep warm.
3 Sauté onion and celery until soft in same kettle. Stir in parsley, salt, thyme, pepper, and cider; heat to boiling. Return chicken pieces; reduce heat; cover. Simmer 45 minutes, or until chicken is tender; remove from heat. Remove chicken pieces from cooking liquid to a heated serving platter; keep hot.
4 Beat egg yolks slightly in a small bowl; blend in light cream. Gradually add cooking liquid, beating vigorously; pour back into saucepan.

Cook, over medium heat, stirring constantly, 1 minute, or until sauce thickens slightly. Pour a little of the sauce over chicken pieces. Pass remaining sauce separately.

Chicken Paprikash
Makes 8 servings

2 broiler-fryers (about 3 pounds each)
2 tablespoons butter or margarine
1 large onion, chopped (1 cup)
2 tablespoons paprika
1 tablespoon flour
3 teaspoons salt
¼ teaspoon pepper
1 can (8 ounces) tomatoes
1 cup (8-ounce carton) dairy sour cream
1 tablespoon chopped parsley
1 package (1 pound) noodles

1 Cut chickens into serving-size pieces.
2 Sauté onion in butter or margarine until soft in a large skillet with a cover. Stir in paprika and flour; cook, stirring constantly, 1 minute. Stir in salt, pepper, and tomatoes (breaking with spoon).
3 Add chicken and giblets (except livers), turning to coat pieces well; cover. Simmer 30 minutes. Turn chicken pieces; add livers; simmer 15 minutes longer, or until chicken is tender.
4 Meanwhile, cook noodles, following label directions; drain; spoon onto hot serving platter. Remove chicken from skillet with a slotted spoon. Arrange on platter with noodles; keep warm.
5 Spoon sour cream into a medium-size bowl. Heat sauce in skillet to boiling; stir slowly into sour cream, blending well. Spoon over chicken.

Chicken, Hunter's Style
Makes 4 servings

1 broiler-fryer (about 3 pounds)
1 tablespoon vegetable oil
1 tablespoon butter or margarine
¼ pound mushrooms, trimmed and sliced
2 large tomatoes, peeled, seeded and chopped
¼ cup sliced green onions
1 small clove of garlic, crushed
¾ cup water
2 tablespoons lemon juice
1 teaspoon leaf chervil or thyme, crumbled
1 teaspoon salt
⅛ teaspoon pepper
1 teaspoon cornstarch

1 Cut chicken into serving-size pieces. Brown

A variation of Chicken Cacciatore—the chicken is cut in bite-size pieces instead of being quartered.

in oil and butter or margarine in a large skillet with a cover.

2 Add mushrooms, tomatoes, green onions, garlic, ½ cup of the water, lemon juice, chervil, salt, and pepper; cover. Simmer 45 minutes, or until chicken is tender. Remove chicken to a heated serving platter; keep hot.

3 Blend cornstarch with remaining water in a cup; stir into liquid in skillet. Cook, stirring constantly, until mixture thickens and bubbles 3 minutes. Pour over chicken; serve at once.

●

Chicken Cacciatore

Men often order this zesty Italian favorite when eating out. It's a good choice, too, for guests, for it waits perfectly.
Makes 8 servings

2 *broiler-fryers (about 3 pounds each), quartered*
¾ *cup unsifted all-purpose flour*
3 *teaspoons salt*
¼ *teaspoon pepper*

6 *tablespoons olive oil or vegetable oil*
1 *large onion, chopped*
1 *clove garlic, minced*
1 *can (about 2 pounds) Italian tomatoes*
1 *tablespoon sugar*
1 *teaspoon leaf basil, crumbled*
½ *teaspoon leaf thyme, crumbled*
2 *medium-size green peppers, halved, seeded, and sliced*

1 Wash chicken quarters; pat dry. Shake with flour, salt, and pepper in a paper bag to coat well.

2 Brown pieces, a few at a time in olive oil or salad oil in a large frying pan; remove all from pan.

3 Stir onion and garlic into drippings in pan and sauté until soft; stir in tomatoes, sugar, basil, and thyme; heat to boiling.

4 Return chicken to pan; spoon some of the tomato sauce over; lay sliced green peppers on top; cover.

5 Simmer, basting several times with sauce in pan, 1½ hours, or until chicken is tender.

153

Twin Chickens Parisiennes

Stuff each with a whole bunch of parsley and simmer in a savory mushroom sauce to serve with noodles.
Makes 6 to 8 servings

2 broiler-fryers (about 3 pounds each)
1 teaspoon salt
½ teaspoon sugar
2 bunches parsley, washed and trimmed
2 tablespoons butter or margarine
1 can (3 or 4 ounces) whole mushrooms
¼ teaspoon pepper
2 tablespoons flour
¾ cup light or table cream
   Hot cooked noodles

1 Rinse chickens inside and out with cold water; drain, then pat dry. Sprinkle insides with ½ teaspoon of the salt and sugar; place parsley in body cavities, packing in lightly. Skewer neck skin to back; twist wing tips flat against skewered neck skin; tie the legs to tails with string.
2 Brown in butter or margarine in a heavy kettle or Dutch oven; turn breast side up.
3 Drain liquid from mushrooms into a 1-cup measure; add water to make ¾ cup; pour over chickens. Sprinkle with remaining ½ teaspoon salt and pepper; cover tightly. (Set mushrooms aside for Step 6.)
4 Simmer, basting several times with liquid in kettle, 1 hour and 15 minutes, or until tender. Remove from kettle and keep hot while making gravy.
5 Pour liquid from kettle into a 2-cup measure; let stand about a minute, or until fat rises to top, then skim off into a cup. Add water to liquid, if needed, to make 1 cup.
6 Measure 2 tablespoonfuls of the fat and return to kettle; blend in flour; stir in the 1 cup liquid. Cook, stirring constantly, until gravy thickens and boils 1 minute. Stir in mushrooms and cream; heat slowly just to boiling. Darken with a few drops bottled gravy coloring, if you wish.
7 Spoon noodles into a heated large serving bowl. Take out skewers and cut strings from chickens; arrange chickens on top of noodles; spoon gravy over all. Garnish with parsley, if you wish. Carve chickens into serving-size pieces.

Chicken Tetrazzini

Makes 6 servings

1 broiler-fryer (2½ to 3 pounds), cut up
1 small onion, peeled and sliced
   Few celery tops
1 teaspoon salt
   Water

1 can (3 or 4 ounces) sliced mushrooms, drained
1 cup thinly sliced celery
1 envelope old-fashioned French salad dressing mix
   Vegetable oil
   Cider vinegar
1 package (8 ounces) thin spaghetti, broken in 1-inch lengths
½ cup light cream or table cream
¾ cup mayonnaise or salad dressing
½ pound Swiss cheese, shredded
2 cups shredded iceberg lettuce

1 Combine chicken, onion, celery tops, salt, and 1 cup water in a medium-size frying pan; cover. Simmer 45 minutes, or until chicken is tender. Remove from broth; cool until easy to handle, then pull off skin and take meat from bones; dice meat. Strain broth and chill for soup another day.
2 Combine chicken with mushrooms and celery in a medium-size bowl.
3 Prepare salad dressing mix with vegetable oil, vinegar, and water, following label directions; drizzle ¼ cup over chicken mixture; toss lightly; chill.
4 Cook spaghetti, following label directions; drain well. While warm, combine with cream and ½ cup of the mayonnaise or salad dressing in a medium-size bowl; toss until evenly coated. Fold in cheese; chill.
5 When ready to serve, place lettuce in a large shallow serving dish; spoon spaghetti mixture on top. Fold remaining ¼ cup mayonnaise or salad dressing into chicken mixture; mound in center of spaghetti. Sprinkle lightly with paprika, if you wish.

Curried Chicken or Turkey

Makes 4 servings

2 tablespoons curry powder
4 tablespoons (½ stick) butter or margarine
3 medium-size onions, chopped (1½ cups)
2 tablespoons flour
½ teaspoon ground ginger
2 chicken bouillon cubes
2 cups water
1 can (about 9 ounces) crushed pineapple
3 cups diced cooked chicken or turkey
2 tablespoons lemon juice
4 cups hot cooked rice

1 Heat curry powder in butter or margarine in large frying pan, stirring often, 2 to 3 minutes. Stir in onions and cook until softened.

2 Blend in flour and ginger, then add bouillon cubes, water, and pineapple and syrup. Heat to boiling, stirring until cubes are dissolved; simmer, uncovered, 5 minutes.

3 Stir in chicken or turkey; cover; simmer 10 minutes longer, or until heated through. Stir in lemon juice; serve over rice.

Paella
Makes 6 servings

- 1 broiler-fryer, (2½ to 3 pounds), cut up
- 1 small onion, peeled and sliced
- 1½ teaspoons salt
- Water
- 1½ cups uncooked regular rice
- 2 tablespoons instant minced onion
- ¼ teaspoon crushed saffron
- 1 envelope French salad dressing mix
- Vegetable oil
- Cider vinegar
- ½ head romaine, separated into leaves
- 2 cans (7 ounces each) minced clams, drained
- ½ pound salami, cubed
- 3 medium-size tomatoes, diced
- 1 jar (6 ounces) marinated artichoke hearts
- 1 can or jar (4 ounces) pimientos, drained and diced
- 1 package (10 ounces) frozen peas, cooked and drained
- ½ cup pitted ripe olives

1 Combine chicken, onion, salt, and 1 cup water in a medium-size frying pan; cover. Simmer 45 minutes, or until chicken is tender. Remove from broth; cool until easy to handle, then pull off skin and take meat from bones; cut into bite-size pieces. Strain broth into a 4-cup measure for next step.

2 Combine rice with instant onion and saffron in a large saucepan; add water to chicken broth to measure amount of liquid called for on rice package; stir into rice. Cook, following label directions. Place in a large bowl.

3 Prepare salad dressing mix with vegetable oil, vinegar, and water, following label directions; fold into rice mixture, then fold in chicken; chill at least an hour to season.

4 When ready to serve, line a large shallow serving dish with romaine.

5 Fold clams, salami, tomatoes, artichoke hearts and liquid, and pimientos into rice mix-

ture; spoon on top of romaine. Spoon peas around edge of rice mixture; tuck olives into peas. Garnish with a large *Pimiento Rose,* if you wish.

PIMIENTO ROSE—Drain liquid from 1 can or jar (4 ounces) whole pimientos. Pat pimientos dry with paper toweling; place on a cutting board. Slit one side of one pimiento from top to bottom and open out flat; roll up tightly, jelly-roll fashion, to form center of rose. Slit remaining pimientos on both sides into two pieces each. Wrap pieces, seed side out and overlapping, around center to form petals.

Chicken Parmigiana
Makes 6 servings

- 3 chicken breasts, (about 12 ounces each), split, skinned, and boned
- 2 eggs, lightly beaten
- 1 teaspoon salt
- ⅛ teaspoon pepper
- ¾ cup fine dry bread crumbs
- ½ cup vegetable oil
- 2 cups tomato sauce
- ¼ teaspoon basil
- ⅛ teaspoon garlic powder
- 1 tablespoon butter or margarine
- ½ cup grated Parmesan cheese
- 8 ounces mozzarella cheese, sliced and cut into triangles

1 Place chicken breasts on cutting board and pound lightly with side of heavy knife or cleaver until about ¼ inch thick.

2 Combine eggs, salt, and pepper. Dip chicken into egg mixture, then crumbs.

3 Heat oil until very hot in a large frying pan. Quickly brown chicken on both sides; remove to shallow baking dish. Pour excess oil from frying pan.

4 Stir tomato sauce, basil, and garlic powder into frying pan; heat to boiling; simmer 10 minutes, or until thickened. Stir in butter or margarine. Pour over chicken; sprinkle with cheese; cover.

5 Bake in moderate oven (350°) 30 minutes; uncover.

6 Place mozzarella over chicken. Bake 10 minutes longer, or until cheese melts.

155

BIRDS OF A FEATHER

Stuffed Boneless Breasts of Chicken
Makes 4 servings

2 cups ready-mix bread stuffing
2 chicken breasts, (about 12 ounces each), split and boned
2 tablespoons butter or margarine, melted
½ teaspoon salt
¼ teaspoon pepper
¼ teaspoon garlic powder
¼ teaspoon paprika
1 can (10½ ounces) condensed cream of mushroom soup
½ cup dry white wine

1 Make stuffing, following label directions.
2 Generously butter a baking dish, 8x8x2. Divide stuffing into 4 equal mounds in baking dish. Top each with a half chicken breast, tucking meat down around stuffing to cover completely. Brush with butter or margarine, sprinkle with salt, pepper, garlic powder, and paprika.
3 Bake in moderate oven (350°) 1 hour, or until golden.
4 Combine soup and wine in a small saucepan; heat slowly, stirring constantly, until bubbly. Pour over chicken and serve.

Asparagus Chicken
Makes 6 servings

3 chicken breasts (about 10 ounces each), skinned and boned
6 tablespoons vegetable oil
½ pound asparagus
1 bunch green onions, trimmed and sliced thin (¾ cup)
1 can (3 or 4 ounces) sliced mushrooms
1 can (10½-ounce) condensed chicken broth
1½ teaspoons ground ginger
1 teaspoon salt
1 teaspoon sugar
¼ teaspoon garlic powder
2 tablespoons cornstarch
⅓ cup dry sherry
3 tablespoons soy sauce
4 cups cooked rice

1 Slice chicken in thin strips about 1½ inches long.
2 Heat 4 tablespoons of the vegetable oil in a large frying pan. Stir in chicken; sauté, stirring several times, 4 minutes, or until chicken turns white. Remove from frying pan to a bowl; keep warm for Step 4.
3 Break tough woody ends from asparagus; wash stalks in cold water. If scales are large or sandy, cut off with a sharp knife, then wash

156

stalks again; drain well. Split each stalk lengthwise, then cut in 1½-inch lengths.
4 Heat remaining 2 tablespoons vegetable oil in same frying pan. Stir in asparagus and onions; sauté 2 minutes. Stir in chicken, mushrooms and liquid, chicken broth, ginger, salt, sugar, and garlic powder; cover. Simmer 3 minutes.
5 Mix cornstarch, sherry, and soy sauce until smooth in a cup; stir into mixture in frying pan. Cook, stirring constantly, until mixture thickens and boils 3 minutes. Serve over rice.

Chafing-Dish Chicken Royale
Perfect for a company buffet. Shrimps and tiny meat balls add the royal touches.
Makes 6 servings

3 chicken breasts (about 12 ounces each), halved
4 cups water
Few celery tops
2½ teaspoons salt
½ pound meat-loaf mixture (ground beef and pork)
6 tablespoons flour
Dash of pepper
1 egg
2 teaspoons grated onion
¼ cup milk
3 medium-size carrots, pared and sliced
1 cup frozen peas (from a 1¼-pound bag)
4 tablespoons (½ stick) butter or margarine
1 tablespoon lemon juice
Few drops liquid red pepper seasoning
1 can (about 5 ounces) deveined shrimps, drained and rinsed
2 tablespoons chopped parsley

1 Combine chicken breasts, water, celery tops, and 2 teaspoons of the salt in a large saucepan; cover. Simmer 30 minutes, or until chicken is tender.
2 Remove from broth and cool until easy to handle. Pull off skin and take meat from bones in one piece; set aside for Step 7. Set broth aside for Step 4.
3 Combine meat-loaf mixture, 2 tablespoons of the flour, remaining ½ teaspoon salt, pepper, egg, onion, and milk in a medium-size bowl; mix with a fork until well-blended. Shape into 18 small balls. (Set remaining flour aside for making sauce.)
4 Reheat chicken broth to boiling; add meat balls; cover. Poach 10 minutes, or until cooked

through; lift out with a slotted spoon and place in a bowl.

5 Cook carrots, covered, in part of the same chicken broth 20 minutes, or until tender; cook peas in remaining broth, following label directions. Drain liquid from each and strain into a 4-cup measure; add more water, if needed, to make 4 cups. Keep carrots and peas hot for Step 7.

6 Melt butter or margarine in a large saucepan; blend in remaining 4 tablespoons flour; cook, stirring constantly, just until bubbly. Stir in the 4 cups chicken broth; continue cooking and stirring until sauce thickens and boils 1 minute. Stir in lemon juice and liquid red pepper seasoning.

7 Cut each half chicken breast into three pieces; add to sauce with meat balls, carrots, and peas. Heat slowly just to boiling; spoon into a chafing dish or heated serving dish. Arrange shrimps on top; sprinkle with parsley.

Molded Chicken Indienne

All white meat blends with curry and chutney for this inviting company-supper mold.
Makes 6 servings

    2 chicken breasts (about 12 ounces each)
3½ cups water
    2 teaspoons salt
    1 teaspoon curry powder
      Few celery tops
    2 envelopes unflavored gelatin
    1 tablespoon sugar
    2 tablespoons lemon juice
 ⅓ cup chutney (from a 6-ounce bottle),
      finely chopped
    1 cup chopped celery

1 Combine chicken breasts with water, salt, curry powder, and celery tops in a large saucepan; cover; simmer 30 minutes, or until tender.

2 Remove chicken from broth; cool until easy to handle. Strain broth into a 4-cup measure; add water, if needed, to make 3½ cups. Pull skin from chicken and take meat from bones; chill meat, then dice.

3 Soften gelatin with sugar in 1 cup of the broth in a medium-size saucepan; heat, stirring constantly, just until gelatin dissolves; remove from heat. Stir in remaining 2½ cups broth.

4 Measure ½ cup of the gelatin mixture into a small bowl; set aside for next step. Stir lemon juice into remaining gelatin in saucepan. Chill about 50 minutes, or until as thick as unbeaten egg white.

5 Stir chutney into gelatin in small bowl; pour into a 6-cup mold; chill about 30 minutes, or just until sticky-firm.

6 Fold chicken and celery into thickened gelatin in saucepan; spoon over sticky-firm chutney layer in mold. Chill several hours, overnight, or until firm.

7 To unmold, run a sharp-tip thin-blade knife around top of mold, then dip *very quickly* in and out of a pan of hot water. Cover mold with serving plate; turn upside down; gently lift off mold. Garnish with leaves of Belgian endive, halved seedless grapes, and flaked coconut, if you wish.

Chicken Kiev

This spectacular, with its parsley-butter stuffing that spills out as you cut each roll, is fussy to make so prepare ahead.
Makes 6 servings

1½ sticks (6 ounces) butter or margarine
  6 chicken breasts (about 12 ounces each)
  4 tablespoons finely chopped parsley
 ½ teaspoon sugar
  2 eggs
  1 cup fine dry bread crumbs
  1 teaspoon salt
 ⅛ teaspoon pepper
    Shortening or vegetable oil for frying

1 Cut butter or margarine into 12 even-length sticks; chill in freezer while fixing chicken, for butter should be *very cold*.

2 Pull skin from chicken breasts; halve breasts and cut meat in one piece from bones. Place each half, boned-side up, between wax paper and pound very thin with a mallet or rolling pin to form a "cutlet." (Be careful not to pound holes in meat.)

3 Place 1 piece very cold butter or margarine, 1 teaspoon parsley, and a dash of the sugar on end of each cutlet; fold sides over to seal in butter, then roll up. Hold in place with wooden picks.

4 Beat eggs slightly in a pie plate; mix bread crumbs, salt, and pepper in a second pie plate. Dip stuffed rolls in egg, then in crumb mixture to coat well. Chill at least an hour. (This much can be done ahead.)

5 When ready to fry, melt enough shortening or pour in enough vegetable oil to make a 2-inch depth in an electric deep-fat fryer or large saucepan; heat to 350°.

6 Fry rolls, 3 to 4 at a time and turning often, 7 minutes, or until tender and crisply golden. Lift out with a slotted spoon; drain well. Keep hot until all rolls are cooked.

157

Grilled Chicken Kebabs
Makes 8 servings

        4 chicken breasts (about 14 ounces each)
            boned
        ½ cup olive oil or vegetable oil
        ¼ cup lime juice
        2 tablespoons grated onion
        1 teaspoon salt
        ¼ teaspoon pepper
        ¼ teaspoon crumbled saffron
        1 tablespoon water
       16 cherry tomatoes
        1 tablespoon butter or margarine, melted
            Hot cooked rice

1 Halve each chicken breast lengthwise, then crosswise. Fold each piece in half, skin side out; thread onto long skewers.
2 Combine olive oil, lime juice, onion, salt, and pepper in a small saucepan. Stir saffron into water in a cup; stir into lime mixture.
3 Place skewers on grill about 10 inches above hot coals; brush chicken with lime mixture.
4 Grill, turning often and brushing with more lime mixture, 45 minutes, or until chicken is tender.
5 About 5 minutes before chicken is cooked, thread cherry tomatoes onto long skewers; brush with melted butter or margarine; place on grill. Heat, turning several times, just until hot. Heat remaining lime mixture in saucepan on edge of grill.
6 Remove chicken and tomatoes from skewers to serving plates. Serve with rice and rest of lime mixture as a dip.

Basic Broiled Chicken
Makes 4 servings

        2 broiler-fryers (about 2 pounds each), halved
            or quartered
            salt and pepper
        ¼ cup (½ stick) melted butter or margarine or
            ¼ cup olive oil or vegetable oil

1 Wash chickens; pat dry. Sprinkle with salt and pepper and brush with melted butter or margarine or with olive or vegetable oil.
2 Place chickens, skin-side down, on rack in broiler pan and broil 6 inches from the heat 20 to 25 minutes, brushing occasionally with the melted butter or margarine or with the oil.

3 Turn chickens, brush with butter, margarine or oil and broil 15 to 20 minutes longer or until nicely browned. *Note:* If chickens brown too quickly, reduce heat or move farther away from broiler unit.

Some Quick Flavor Variations:
    Garlic-Broiled Chicken: Warm ½ crushed clove garlic with ¼ cup melted butter or margarine 3 to 5 minutes to mellow flavors; broil chickens as directed, brushing with the garlic butter.
    Lemon-Broiled Chicken: Mix the juice of ½ lemon with ¼ cup melted butter or margarine; broil chickens as directed, brushing with the lemon butter.
    Orange-Broiled Chicken: Warm 1 to 2 tablespoons tart orange marmalade with ¼ cup melted butter or margarine 3 to 5 minutes; broil chickens as directed, brushing with the orange butter.
    Chili-Broiled Chicken: Warm 1 teaspoon chili powder, ½ crushed clove garlic and ⅛ teaspoon cayenne pepper with ¼ cup melted butter or margarine 3 to 5 minutes until no raw chili powder taste remains; broil chickens as directed, brushing with the chili mixture.
    Curry-Broiled Chicken: Warm 1 to 2 tablespoons curry powder, ¼ crushed clove garlic and 1 tablespoon finely minced chutney with ¼ cup melted butter or margarine 3 to 5 minutes until no raw curry taste remains; broil chickens as directed brushing with the curry mixture.

Mandarin Chicken Breasts
Makes 6 servings

        6 chicken breasts (about 12 ounces each),
            boned
            Salt
     1½ cups hot cooked rice
        3 tablespoons butter or margarine
        1 tablespoon chopped parsley
        ¼ teaspoon leaf rosemary, crumbled
        ¼ teaspoon leaf basil, crumbled
        ¼ cup unsifted all-purpose flour
        ½ teaspoon paprika
        2 envelopes instant chicken broth or 2 tea-
            spoons granulated chicken bouillon
     1¾ cups water
        1 tablespoon instant minced onion
        2 tablespoons lemon juice
        1 bay leaf
        1 tablespoon cornstarch
        1 can (about 11 ounces) mandarin orange
            segments, drained
        1 cup seedless green grapes

1 Sprinkle insides of chicken breasts lightly with salt.

Mandarin Chicken Breasts are just as good as they look.

2 Combine rice, 1 tablespoon of the butter or margarine, ¼ teaspoon salt, parsley, rosemary, and basil in a large bowl; toss lightly to mix; spoon into hollows in chicken breasts. Fold edges over stuffing to cover completely; fasten with wooden picks.

3 Mix flour, paprika, and ½ teaspoon salt in a pie plate; dip chicken breasts into mixture to coat well. Brown slowly in remaining 2 tablespoons butter or margarine in a large frying pan.

4 Stir in chicken broth, water, onion, lemon juice, and bay leaf; heat to boiling; cover.

5 Simmer 25 minutes, or until chicken is tender; remove bay leaf. Place chicken on a heated deep serving platter; keep warm. Reheat liquid to boiling.

6 Smooth cornstarch with a little water to a paste in a cup; stir into liquid in frying pan. Cook, stirring constantly, until sauce thickens and boils 3 minutes. Stir in mandarin orange segments and grapes; heat until bubbly. Spoon over chicken. Garnish with additional grapes and mandarin-orange segments threaded onto a long skewer.

Just-Right Fried Chicken

This is the kind of fried chicken that will boost your fame handsomely high. Cook it slowly (it just can't be hurried) and it will come out with the crispest golden jacket hiding the tenderest sweet meat—every time.

Buy plump broiler-fryers weighing about 3 pounds each. Cut each into 8 serving-size pieces—2 breasts, 2 wings, 2 thighs, 2 drumsticks. Simmer bony back pieces to make broth for gravy, if you wish. To coat and season each chicken you'll need:

½ *cup unsifted all-purpose flour*
1 *teaspoon salt*
⅛ *teaspoon pepper*
And for frying:
1 *cup bacon drippings or part drippings and*
   shortening

1 Wash chicken, but do not dry. This is important so skin will take on a thick flour coating. Mix flour, salt, and pepper in a bag. Shake pieces, a few at a time, to coat evenly all over
2 Heat a quarter-inch depth bacon drippings in an electric skillet to 360°, or use a large heavy frying pan on medium heat. Arrange chicken, without crowding, in a single layer in hot fat
3 Brown slowly for 15 minutes. When pink juices start to show on top, turn and brown the other side 15 minutes. It's the slow cooking, plus *turning just once,* that gives chicken its crisp coating
4 When pieces are browned, pile all into skillet and cover. Reset control at 260°, or lower range heat to simmer. Let chicken cook 20 minutes longer, or until it's richly golden and fork-tender

Country Fried Chicken

Country Fried Chicken
Nothing quite equals crispy-brown fried chicken in popularity—and here's how.
Makes 6 to 8 servings

2 *broiler-fryers (about 2 pounds each), cut into*
   serving-size pieces
⅔ *cup unsifted all-purpose flour*
2 *teaspoons salt*
1 *teaspoon paprika*
¼ *teaspoon pepper*
1 *cup bacon drippings*
2 *cloves of garlic*
1 *bay leaf*
   Milk Gravy (recipe follows)

1 Wash and dry chicken pieces. Shake, a few at a time, in mixture of flour, salt, paprika, and pepper in paper bag to coat well.
2 Heat bacon drippings with whole cloves of garlic and bay leaf in electric skillet, following manufacturer's directions for fried chicken.
3 Place chicken in single layer in hot drippings. (Do not crowd as pieces should have enough room to brown without touching each other.) Cook slowly, turning once or twice to brown both sides. (It will take about 30 minutes.)

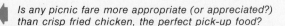
Is any picnic fare more appropriate (or appreciated?) than crisp fried chicken, the perfect pick-up food?

4 Return all chicken to skillet; cover; cook slowly 20 minutes, or until tender. Uncover; cook 5 minutes longer to crisp coating. Remove chicken to heated platter; keep hot while making gravy.
   Milk Gravy—Tip skillet and pour off all drippings into a cup, leaving crusty brown bits in skillet. (Be sure to remove cloves of garlic and bay leaf.) Return 3 tablespoons drippings to skillet; blend in 3 tablespoons flour; cook, stirring all the time, just until mixture bubbles. Stir in 1 cup water and 1 cup milk slowly; continue cooking and stirring, scraping brown bits from bottom and sides of skillet, until gravy thickens and boils 1 minute. Season to taste with salt. Makes about 2 cups.

Dunkin' Chicken
It's finger-food—crackly-crisp outside, juicy all the way through.
Makes 6 servings

2 *broiler-fryers (about 2 pounds each), cut up*
1 *cup unsifted all-purpose flour*
2 *teaspoons salt*
½ *teaspoon pepper*
   Bacon drippings for frying
   Orange-curry Dunk (recipe follows)
   Zippy Tomato Dunk (recipe follows)

1 Wash and dry chicken pieces well. Shake in mixture of flour, salt, and pepper in paper bag to coat well.
2 Heat bacon drippings in large heavy frying pan or electric skillet. It'll take about 1 cup, for fat should be about ½ inch deep. (If you like, use part shortening or vegetable oil.)

161

3 Place chicken in single layer in hot fat; cover lightly. Cook over *low heat* 20 minutes, or until golden; turn; cover again and cook 20 minutes to brown other side. (If using an electric skillet, follow manufacturer's directions.) Remove browned chicken and set aside while cooking any remaining pieces, adding more drippings, if needed, to keep fat ½ inch deep.

4 Drain fat from frying pan, leaving just enough to keep chicken from sticking; return all chicken to pan. Cover; cook, turning once or twice, over *very low heat* 30 minutes longer, or until chicken is tender.

5 Serve hot or cold, plain or with dunking sauces.

Orange-Curry Dunk
Just sweet, just tart enough to go with mild-flavor chicken.
Makes 2 cups

  1 cup orange marmalade
  ⅓ cup vinegar
  ¼ cup granulated sugar
  2 tablespoons brown sugar
  1 tablespoon curry powder
  1 tablespoon Worcestershire sauce
  1 teaspoon salt
  ½ teaspoon ground ginger

Combine all ingredients in small saucepan; heat to boiling, then simmer, stirring constantly, until marmalade is melted and sauce is blended. Serve warm or cold.

Zippy Tomato Dunk
It's tomato-rich and spicy—a good all-round sauce to keep on hand.
Makes 1½ cups

  1 can (8 ounces) tomato sauce
  ½ cup finely chopped green pepper
  ½ cup finely chopped celery
  2 tablespoons vinegar
  2 tablespoons light molasses
  1 tablespoon Worcestershire sauce
  ¼ teaspoon liquid red pepper seasoning

Combine all ingredients in small saucepan; heat to boiling, then simmer, stirring constantly, 5 minutes, or until vegetables are softened and sauce is blended. Serve warm or cold.

Drumstick Fricassee
Lemon-flecked dumpling puffs steam atop meaty chicken legs, sweet potatoes, and peas in rich gravy.
Makes 2 servings

  4 chicken drumsticks (about 1 pound)
  ½ small onion, sliced
  ¼ cup chopped celery tops
  1 teaspoon salt
  ⅛ teaspoon pepper
  1½ cups water
  2 teaspoons flour
  1 large sweet potato, pared and sliced ½ inch thick
  1 cup frozen peas (from a 1½-pound bag)
  Lemon Dumplings (recipe follows)

Cook chicken with onion, celery tops, salt, and pepper in 1 cup of the water 30 minutes, or until tender. Blend flour into remaining ½ cup water; stir into broth; cook, stirring constantly, until gravy thickens and boils 1 minute. Add potato and peas; heat to boiling, then simmer 10 minutes while making *Lemon Dumplings.* Drop batter in 4 mounds on top of hot chicken and vegetables; cover tightly. Cook 20 minutes, or until dumplings are fluffy-light. Lift off dumplings; spoon chicken, vegetables, and gravy into serving dishes; top with dumplings. Garnish with grated lemon rind, if you wish.

Lemon Dumplings
Fluffy, light, and fragrant with lemon.

Combine ⅔ cup sifted all-purpose flour, 1 teaspoon baking powder, ½ teaspoon grated lemon rind, and ¼ teaspoon salt. Stir 1 teaspoon lemon juice into ⅓ cup milk. (No need to fuss if mixture curdles.) Add all at once to dry ingredients; stir just until flour mixture is moistened completely.

Jellied Chicken
A perfect make-ahead and wonderful eating on a hot summer day.
Makes 6 to 8 servings

  1 stewing chicken (5 to 6 pounds), not cut up
  1 medium-size onion, sliced
  2 teaspoons salt
  1 teaspoon peppercorns
  Handful of celery tops

2½ cups water
1 envelope unflavored gelatin
2 hard-cooked eggs, shelled and sliced
  Parsley
1 tablespoon prepared mustard
½ cup dairy sour cream

1 Simmer chicken with onion, salt, peppercorns, celery tops, and water in large kettle, covered, 2 hours, or until tender. Let stand in broth until cool enough to handle.
2 Strain broth into a 4-cup measure; skim off any fat that rises to top, then add water, if needed, to make 3 cups; cool.
3 Pull all chicken from frame; trim off any fat and skin; chop meat fine. (You should have about 4 cups.) Spoon into a 6-cup loaf pan.
4 Soften gelatin in 1 cup of the cooled broth in small saucepan; heat, stirring constantly, just until dissolved. Stir back into remaining broth; pour over chicken in loaf pan, pressing chicken down with a fork until completely covered (mixture should just fill pan).

5 Chill 5 to 6 hours or overnight, or until the loaf is firm enough to cut into neat slices.
6 Unmold onto serving plate; garnish with sliced hard-cooked eggs and parsley. Slice and serve with prepared mustard blended into the sour cream.

●

Chicken Livers Greek Style
Specially flavored chicken livers combine with tender eggplant for a different dinner idea.
Makes 6 servings

1 eggplant (about 1 pound), sliced ½ inch thick
5 tablespoons flour
1 teaspoon salt
2 tablespoons vegetable oil
4 tablespoons (½ stick) butter or margarine
1½ pounds chicken livers, washed and cut in half
1 medium-size onion, sliced
½ teaspoon leaf basil, crumbled
1 can (10½ ounces) condensed chicken broth

Drumstick Fricassee, the sort of homely, hearty old-fashioned recipe that can warm the soul as well as the body on a wintry day.

2 *tomatoes, peeled and cut in eighths*
2 *tablespoons chopped parsley*

1 Dip eggplant slices in mixture of 3 tablespoons of the flour and salt. Sauté in oil and 2 tablespoons of butter or margarine about 3 minutes on each side, or until soft in a large skillet. Arrange, overlapping, as a border around edge of heated serving dish. Keep warm.
2 Sauté chicken livers and onion in remaining butter or margarine in same skillet 6 minutes, or until browned. Stir in remaining 2 tablespoons flour and basil. Gradually stir in broth.
3 Heat, stirring constantly, until mixture thickens and bubbles 1 minute. Add tomatoes; cover; reduce heat; simmer 5 minutes. Spoon into center of serving dish with eggplant border. Sprinkle with parsley and serve with hot cooked rice, if you wish.

Chicken Livers With Bacon Crisps

Do try this oven way to cook delicate liver to perfection.
Bake at 400° for 30 minutes. Makes 6 servings

12 *slices (about ½ pound) bacon*
 1 *pound chicken livers*
 4 *tablespoons flour*
 1 *teaspoon salt*
 ½ *teaspoon paprika*
 6 *slices hot toast*
   Pepper

1 Lay bacon slices in single layer on rack of broiler pan. (If slices don't separate easily, heat in oven for a few minutes.) Bake in hot oven (400°) 10 minutes, or until crisp. (No need to turn.) Remove rack with bacon on it; keep warm. (Leave oven heat on.)
2 Shake chicken livers in mixture of flour, salt, and paprika in paper bag to coat well; lay in hot drippings in broiler pan.
3 Bake in hot oven (400°) 10 minutes, or until browned on underside; turn; bake 10 minutes longer, or until browned on other side. Drain on paper toweling.
4 Arrange toast slices in single layer on heated large serving platter; brush very lightly with bacon drippings from broiler pan. Arrange livers on top; sprinkle with pepper; top with criss-crossed bacon slices.

164

TURKEY

Basic Roast Turkey

Roast at 325° from 4 to 4½ hours. Makes 12 servings

 1 *cleaned fresh or frozen turkey (about 12 to 14 pounds)*
   Salt (plain or seasoned)
12 *cups any favorite poultry stuffing (see Some Favorite Poultry Stuffings that follow)*
 6 *tablespoons (¾ stick) butter or margarine, melted*

1 Sprinkle inside of bird lightly with plain or seasoned salt, then lightly stuff neck cavity. Smooth neck skin over stuffing and skewer to back of bird. Twist wing tips until they rest flat against skewered neck skin.
2 Stuff body cavity, taking care not to pack the stuffing (it needs room to expand as it cooks). If turkey comes "tucked" (with legs slipped under a ribbon-like skin band across opening), slide legs out, stuff lightly, then slip legs back in place. If turkey is not a "tucked" type, lace opening together with poultry pins or skewers and string and truss legs close to body.
3 Brush stuffed bird all over with melted butter or margarine, place, breast-side up, in roasting pan—on a rack, if you wish—but do not cover pan or add any water. If using a meat thermometer, stick it into the center of a thigh without touching bone.
4 Roast in a slow oven (325°) for time suggested on turkey wrapper or about 4 hours for a 12-pounder or until thermometer registers 185°. After bird has been in the oven about 30 minutes, brush again with melted butter. During rest of roasting time, baste every half hour with buttery drippings in pan.
5 Start testing for doneness 30 minutes before roasting time is up. Protecting your fingers with paper toweling, squeeze meaty part of thigh. It should feel soft. Now move drumstick up and down. It should twist and move easily.
6 When turkey is done, remove strings and skewers, place on a heated platter and keep warm while making *Giblet Gravy* or *Onion-Mushroom Gravy* (both recipes are included in this section) or your own favorite gravy.
Note: Turkey will carve more neatly if allowed to stand 15 to 20 minutes beforehand.

Golden Twin Turkeys

Roast at 325° about 2½ hours. Makes 8 servings, plus enough for another meal

Basic Roast Turkey, the bigger and browner the better, laid out on a properly festive, properly groaning board.

A double Thanksgiving treat—two roast turkeys instead of one mean double the drumsticks, thighs and breasts.

2 cleaned fresh or frozen turkeys (about 6 pounds each)
Salt
8 cups any favorite poultry stuffing or 4 cups each of 2 different stuffings (see Some Favorite Poultry Stuffings that follow)
1 can (10½ ounces) condensed beef broth
½ cup (1 stick) butter or margarine

1 Sprinkle insides of birds with salt, then lightly stuff neck cavities. Smooth neck skins over stuffing and skewer to backs of birds. Twist wing tips until they rest flat against skewered neck skins.

2 Stuff body cavities, taking care not to pack the stuffing. If turkeys come "tucked" (with legs slipped under a ribbon-like skin band across opening), slide legs out, stuff lightly, then slip legs back in place. If turkeys are not the "tucked" type, lace openings together with poultry pins or skewers and string and truss legs close to bodies.

3 Place birds, breast-side up and side by side, not touching, on a rack in a large roasting pan. Do not cover pan or add any water. Insert meat

166

thermometer into the thickest part of a thigh without touching bone.

4 Heat beef broth and butter or margarine in a small saucepan just until butter or margarine melts. Brush part over turkeys to coat well.

5 Roast turkeys in a slow oven (325°), brushing every half hour with remaining broth mixture, 2½ hours, or until thermometer registers 185°.

6 Start testing for doneness 30 minutes before roasting time is up. Protecting your fingers with paper toweling, squeeze the meaty part of a thigh. It should feel soft. Now move a drumstick up and down. It should twist and move easily.

7 When turkeys are done, remove strings and skewers, place on a heated serving platter and let stand 15 to 20 minutes before carving. *Note:* This is a good time to make gravy—*Giblet or Onion-Mushroom Gravy* (both recipes are included in this section) or your own favorite gravy.

Cranberry-Glazed Roast Turkey
Pop a frozen ready-stuffed bird into a pan, roast, and glaze—it's that simple.

Turkey needn't be confined to the Thanksgiving table; the big birds come frozen, can be enjoyed year round.

Roast at 325° about 6 hours. Makes 8 servings, plus enough for another meal

1 frozen stuffed turkey (about 10 pounds)
½ cup (1 stick) butter or margarine, softened
1 can (7 ounces) jellied cranberry sauce
1 teaspoon Worcestershire sauce
½ teaspoon leaf marjoram, crumbled

1 Remove frozen stuffed turkey from wrapper; place turkey, breast up, on a rack in a roasting pan; coat with soft butter or margarine.
2 Roast, following label directions for turkey cooked in an uncovered pan, and basting every hour with buttery drippings in pan, 5½ hours.
3 Pour off all drippings into a small bowl; measure 2 tablespoonfuls into a small saucepan; set remaining aside for making gravy, if you wish.
4 Stir cranberry and Worcestershire sauces and marjoram into drippings in saucepan; heat, stirring constantly, just to boiling. Brush part over turkey.
5 Continue roasting, basting several times with remaining cranberry mixture, 30 minutes longer,

or until drumstick feels very soft and a meat thermometer inserted into center of stuffing registers 165°.
6 Remove turkey to a heated platter; carve and serve. After serving, remove any leftover stuffing from turkey and chill separately.

NOTE—If you wish to make gravy, fix it in another pan, as the cranberry drippings in the roasting pan tend to make the gravy too sweet.

●

167

Roast Turkey Breast With Chestnut Stuffing
Roast at 325° for 2½ hours. Makes about 8 servings

1 medium-size onion, chopped
½ cup diced celery
½ cup (1 stick) butter or margarine
1 tablespoon parsley flakes
1½ teaspoons leaf thyme, crumbled
1 teaspoon salt
¼ teaspoon pepper
1 cup coarsely chopped canned chestnuts
⅓ cup water

6 slices white bread, toasted and cut in tiny cubes (3 cups)
1 frozen turkey breast (about 5 pounds), thawed

1 Sauté onion and celery in ¼ cup of the butter or margarine until soft in a medium-size frying pan. Stir in parsley, thyme, salt, pepper, chestnuts, and water; heat to boiling. Pour over bread in a large bowl; toss until evenly moist.

2 Turn turkey breast upside down on a cutting board; spread open. Lightly stuff chestnut mixture into neck and breast cavities. Fold sides of breast up over stuffing; hold in place with skewers. Smooth neck skin over stuffing; skewer. Place roast, skin side up, on a rack in a shallow roasting pan.

3 Melt remaining ¼ cup butter or margarine in a small saucepan; brush over turkey. Insert meat thermometer into thickest part of breast without touching bone. Cover pan loosely with foil.

4 Roast in slow oven (325°) 1½ hours; uncover. Continue roasting, brushing turkey several times with drippings in pan, 1 hour longer, or until turkey is tender and thermometer registers 185°.

5 Place turkey on a heated serving platter; remove skewers. Surround with sautéed mushrooms and buttered whole green beans, if you wish.

Giblet Gravy

With broth ready ahead of time, gravy goes together quickly.
Makes about 4 cups

Turkey giblets (except liver and neck)
1 medium-size onion, chopped
Few celery tops
1 teaspoon salt
1 bay leaf
4 cups water
Turkey liver
8 tablespoons turkey fat
½ cup sifted all-purpose flour
Salt and pepper to season

1 Combine giblets, onion, celery tops, 1 teaspoon salt, bay leaf and 4 cups water in a medium-size saucepan. Simmer 1 hour and 40 minutes; add liver, simmer 20 minutes longer or until meat is tender.

2 Strain broth; measure; add water, if necessary, to make 4 cups.

3 Chop giblets fine and stir into broth. Cool, then chill until ready to make gravy.

4 After turkey has been removed from roasting pan, remove rack, if used; tip pan and let fat rise in one corner. Pour all fat into a cup leaving juices in pan. Measure 8 tablespoons fat and return to pan; blend in flour. Cook, stirring constantly, just until bubbly.

5 Stir in 4 cups giblet broth and giblets; continue cooking and stirring, scraping baked-on juices from bottom and sides of pan, until gravy thickens and boils 1 minute.

6 Season to taste with salt and pepper; stir in a little bottled gravy coloring to darken, if you wish.

Onion-Mushroom Gravy

Onion soup mix richens the savory broth for this variation of a holiday-dinner must.
Makes about 4 cups

Turkey giblets
1 bay leaf
3½ cups water
1 envelope onion soup mix
8 tablespoons turkey drippings
½ cup sifted all-purpose flour
1 can (6 ounces) sliced mushrooms

1 Combine turkey giblets (except liver) and necks with bay leaf and water in a medium-size saucepan. Heat to boiling; stir in soup mix.

2 Simmer 40 minutes; add livers. Simmer 20 minutes longer, or until giblets are tender. Remove from broth and chill to dice for soup for another day. Measure broth and add water, if needed, to make 3½ cups.

3 After turkeys have been removed from roasting pan, remove rack, if used. Tip pan and let drippings rise in one corner, then pour off into a cup, leaving juices in pan. Measure the 8 tablespoons drippings and return to pan.

4 Blend in flour; cook, stirring constantly, until bubbly. Stir in the 3½ cups broth and mushrooms and liquid. Continue cooking and stirring, scraping baked-on juices from bottom and sides of pan, until gravy thickens and boils 1 minute. Stir in a few drops bottled gravy coloring to darken, if you wish, and season with salt and pepper, if needed.

A savory stuffing makes the roast turkey (or chicken, duck, game hen or goose). There's good variety here.

SOME FAVORITE POULTRY STUFFINGS

For directions on How to Stuff and Truss Poultry, see the introductory pages of BIRDS OF A FEATHER.

NOTE: Any stuffing left over after bird is stuffed can be wrapped in foil or spooned into a buttered baking dish, covered, and baked alongside bird during final hour of roasting.

Herb Stuffing
Makes about 10 cups, or enough to stuff a 12-pound turkey

    1 large onion, chopped
    1 cup (2 sticks) butter or margarine
    1 cup finely chopped celery
    2 envelopes instant chicken broth or 2 tea-
       spoons granulated chicken bouillon

    1 teaspoon poultry seasoning
    ½ teaspoon salt
    ¼ teaspoon seasoned pepper
    1¼ cups water
    12 cups cubed white bread (24 slices)
    ¾ cup chopped parsley

1 Sauté onion in butter or margarine until soft in a medium-size frying pan; stir in celery, chicken broth, poultry seasoning, salt, pepper, and water; heat to boiling.
2 Pour over bread and parsley in a large bowl; toss lightly until evenly moist.

Double Rice Stuffing
Makes about 10 cups, or enough to stuff a 12-pound turkey

    2 packages (6 ounces each) long-grain and
       wild-rice mix
    6 tablespoons (¾ stick) butter or margarine
    4½ cups water
    3 cups chopped celery
    1 large onion, chopped

169

1 jar (7 ounces) pimiento-stuffed olives,
   drained and sliced
1 teaspoon salt
¼ teaspoon pepper

1 Prepare rice mix with 2 tablespoons of the butter or margarine and the 4½ cups water, following label directions.
2 Sauté celery and onion in remaining butter or margarine until soft in a large frying pan; lightly stir in rice mixture, olives, salt, and pepper.

Brown Rice Stuffing

Makes about 10 cups, or enough to stuff a 12-pound turkey

 9 cups water
 1 tablespoon salt
 3 cups brown rice (1½ boxes, 12 ounces each)
 2 cups chopped celery
 1 medium-size onion, grated
 ½ cup (1 stick) butter or margarine
 ½ cup chopped parsley
 2 teaspoons salt
1½ teaspoons poultry seasoning

1 Combine water and the 1 tablespoon salt in a kettle. Heat to boiling. Stir in rice; reduce heat; cover. Simmer 45 minutes, or until rice is tender. Drain; place in a large bowl.
2 Sauté celery and onion in butter or margarine until soft in a medium-size skillet. Stir in parsley, the remaining 2 teaspoons salt, and poultry seasoning.
3 Pour over rice; stir lightly until evenly mixed.

Mushroom Stuffing

Makes about 10 cups, or enough to stuff a 12-pound turkey

 1 pound fresh mushrooms
10 bunches green onions
 1 cup (2 sticks) butter or margarine
12 cups coarse soft white-bread crumbs (24 slices)
 1 teaspoon salt

1 Wash mushrooms and trim; chop caps and stems. (There will be about 5½ cups.)
2 Trim onions and slice. (There will be about 6 cups.)

3 Sauté mushrooms and onions in butter or margarine in a large frying pan 10 minutes, or just until wilted. Pour over bread crumbs in a large bowl; sprinkle with salt; toss lightly until evenly moist.

Sausage and Apple Stuffing

Makes about 10 cups, or enough to stuff a 12-pound turkey

 8 cups cubed white bread (16 slices)
 1 pound sausage meat
 1 large onion, diced
 2 large apples, pared, quartered, cored, and chopped
½ cup water
 1 teaspoon salt

1 Spread bread cubes on large cooky sheets; place in very slow oven (250°) 10 minutes; remove from oven; reserve.
2 Cut sausage into 8 thick slices. Brown 5 minutes on each side in a medium-size skillet, then break into small pieces. Cook 1 minute longer, or until no trace of pink remains. Combine with bread cubes in a large bowl.
3 Pour off drippings from skillet; measure; return 2 tablespoons. Add onions and sauté until tender. Stir in water and apples; heat to boiling. Pour over sausage mixture; add salt; toss lightly until evenly moist.

Dixie Belle Stuffing

Makes about 10 cups, or enough to stuff a 12-pound turkey

 1 pound sausage meat
 2 packages (8 ounces each) ready-mix corn-bread stuffing
 2 large onions, diced
 2 cups diced celery
1¼ cups water
 ½ cup chopped parsley

1 Cut sausage in 8 thick slices. Brown 5 minutes on each side in a medium-size frying pan, then break in small chunks. Cook 1 minute longer, or until no pink remains. Remove with a slotted spoon and combine with stuffing mix in a large bowl.
2 Stir onions and celery into drippings in pan; sauté until soft. Stir in water; heat to boiling. Pour over sausage mixture; add parsley; toss lightly until evenly moist.

Peanut Stuffing

Makes about 10 cups, or enough to stuff a 12-pound turkey

    1 medium-size onion, chopped
    2 cups chopped celery
    ¾ cup (1½ sticks) butter or margarine
 2½ cups water
    2 packages (7 ounces each) seasoned stuff-
       ing croutons
    1 cup salted peanuts, ground fine

1 Sauté onion and celery in butter or margarine until soft in a large frying pan. Stir in water; heat to boiling.
2 Pour over croutons and peanuts in a large bowl; toss until evenly moist.

Sausage Stuffing

Here's an old-time favorite for those who prefer a spicy meat dressing.
Makes about 6 cups, or enough to stuff an 8-pound turkey

    ½ pound sausage meat
    4 cups cubed slightly dry white bread (8
       slices)
    2 tablespoons milk
    1 cup diced celery
    ½ teaspoon salt
    ½ teaspoon poultry seasoning
    ⅛ teaspoon pepper

1 Brown sausage slowly in a small frying pan, breaking meat up with a fork as it cooks; remove with a slotted spoon and place in a medium-size bowl. Add bread cubes; drizzle with milk.
2 Stir celery into drippings in pan; sauté until soft; stir in salt, poultry seasoning, and pepper.
3 Pour over bread mixture; toss until evenly moist.

Raisin-Walnut Stuffing

Makes 10 cups, or enough to stuff a 12-pound turkey

    2 cups seedless raisins
 1½ cups water
    2 cups chopped celery
    1 large onion, chopped
    ½ cup (1 stick) butter or margarine
    1 envelope instant chicken broth or 1 tea-
       spoon granulated chicken bouillon

    1 teaspoon salt
    1 teaspoon powdered sage
    ¼ teaspoon pepper
    8 cups cubed white bread (16 slices)
    2 cups coarsely chopped walnuts

1 Simmer raisins in water in a small saucepan for 1 minute; reserve.
2 Sauté celery and onion in butter or margarine until soft in a large skillet. Stir in chicken broth, salt, sage, and pepper.
3 Add to bread cubes and walnuts in a large bowl; add raisin-water mixture; toss lightly until evenly moist.

German Potato Stuffing

Variation on an old-time recipe calls for lots of raw potatoes, subtle seasonings.
Makes about 12 cups, or enough to stuff a 12- to 14-pound turkey

    ½ cup shortening
    8 tablespoons (1 stick) butter or margarine
  16 large potatoes, pared and diced (about 16
       cups)
    3 large onions, chopped
    1 cup thinly sliced celery
    4 teaspoons salt
    ½ teaspoon pepper
    ½ cup milk
    3 cups coarse slightly dry white-bread crumbs
       (6 slices)
    4 eggs
    6 tablespoons chopped parsley

1 Melt shortening and butter or margarine in a large frying pan.
2 Stir in potatoes, onions, celery, salt, and pepper; cover loosely.
3 Cook slowly, stirring often, 30 minutes, or until potatoes are tender.
4 Pour milk over bread crumbs in a small bowl; stir into potato mixture, then stir in eggs. Continue cooking, stirring constantly, until eggs are cooked. (Flecks of cooked egg will show in the stuffing.) Remove from heat.
5 Stir in parsley. Cool slightly.

171

Parsley-Egg Stuffing

Chopped hard-cooked egg and chicken broth delicately season bread stuffing.
Makes about 12 cups, or enough to stuff a 12- to 14-pound turkey

BIRDS OF A FEATHER

1 large onion, chopped
½ cup (1 stick) butter or margarine
1 envelope instant chicken broth
  OR: 1 chicken bouillon cube
1½ teaspoons salt
1 cup water
10 cups cubed slightly dry white bread (about 20 slices)
3 hard-cooked eggs, shelled and chopped
½ cup chopped parsley

1 Sauté onion in butter or margarine until soft in a small frying pan; stir in chicken broth or bouillon cube, salt, and water. Heat to boiling, crushing bouillon cube, if used, with spoon.
2 Pour over bread cubes in a large bowl; toss lightly until evenly moist. Fold in eggs and parsley.

Southwest Corn Bread Stuffing
Makes about 6 cups, or enough to stuff the neck cavity of a 12-pound turkey

1 cup chopped celery
1 large onion, chopped
½ cup (1 stick) butter or margarine
1 teaspoon chili powder
1 package (8 ounces) ready-mix corn bread stuffing
¼ cup chopped pimiento-stuffed olives
1 egg
⅓ cup water

1 Sauté celery and onion in butter or margarine until soft in a large skillet. Stir in chili powder; cook 1 minute longer. Remove from heat; stir in stuffing mix and olives.
2 Beat egg slightly with water in a small bowl; pour over stuffing mixture in skillet; toss lightly until evenly moist.

172

Chestnut-Celery Stuffing
Makes 3 cups, or enough to stuff the neck cavity of a 6-pound turkey

¾ pound fresh chestnuts
1 cup cubed white bread (2 slices)
½ cup diced celery
1 small onion, chopped
2 tablespoons butter or margarine

1 can (3 or 4 ounces) chopped mushrooms
¾ teaspoon salt
⅛ teaspoon pepper
½ teaspoon poultry seasoning

1 Wash chestnuts; cut slits in each shell; place in a shallow baking pan. Bake in very hot oven (475°) 15 minutes. Remove chestnuts; lower oven temperature to very slow (250°). When cool enough to handle, shell and skin nuts.
2 Cook, covered, in boiling salted water to cover, in a medium-size saucepan, about 15 minutes, or until tender; drain; chop fine. (You should have about 1½ cups.)
3 While chestnuts are cooking, spread bread cubes on a large cooky sheet; place in very slow (250°) oven 10 minutes; remove from oven; reserve.
4 Sauté celery and onion in butter or margarine just until soft in a medium-size skillet. Combine with chestnuts in a medium-size bowl.
5 Add mushrooms and their liquid, salt, pepper, bread cubes, and poultry seasoning; toss lightly until evenly moist.

Vegetable Stuffing
Parsley, olives, and water chestnuts go with ready-seasoned croutons for this mild moist dressing.
Makes about 6 cups, or enough to stuff an 8-pound turkey

1 large onion, chopped
4 tablespoons (½ stick) butter or margarine
¼ cup chopped parsley
2 tablespoons chopped stuffed green olives
6 water chestnuts (from a 5-ounce can), chopped
¼ cup hot water
4 cups herb-seasoned stuffing croutons (from a 7-ounce package)

1 Sauté onion in butter or margarine until soft in a small frying pan; stir in parsley, olives, water chestnuts, and water.
2 Pour over croutons in a medium-size bowl; toss until evenly moist.

Scalloped Corn Stuffing
Makes about 4 cups, or enough to stuff a 6-pound turkey

Turkeys can weigh anything from four to 30 pounds. This fellow's a heavy-weight for big-family feasts.

1 can (12 or 16 ounces) whole-kernel corn
1 package (about 4 ounces) unsalted soda
   crackers, coarsely crushed
¼ cup chopped parsley
1 medium-size onion, chopped
½ cup thinly sliced celery
4 tablespoons (½ stick) butter or margarine
¼ cup light cream or table cream
1 teaspoon salt
⅛ teaspoon pepper
2 eggs, beaten

1 Drain liquid from corn into a cup. Combine corn, crackers, and parsley in a large bowl.
2 Sauté onion and celery in butter or margarine until soft in a small saucepan; stir in ¼ cup of the corn liquid, cream, salt, and pepper. Pour over cracker mixture; add eggs; toss lightly until evenly moist.

Apple Stuffing
Makes about 4 cups, or enough to stuff a 6-pound turkey

1 large apple, pared, quartered, cored, and
   chopped
1 medium-size onion, chopped
2 tablespoons butter or margarine
1 envelope instant chicken broth or 1 teaspoon
   granulated chicken bouillon
¼ cup water
½ teaspoon leaf rosemary, crumbled
5 cups toasted bread cubes

1 Sauté apple and onion in butter or margarine until soft in a small frying pan.
2 Stir in chicken broth, water, and rosemary; heat to boiling. Pour over bread cubes in a large bowl; toss lightly until evenly moist.

173

174

1 Place bird on platter with the drumsticks to carver's right. Holding onto leg, bend it down toward platter while cutting through thigh joint to separate the whole piece from frame; set it aside.

2 Stick fork into bird near the breastbone and, with other hand, cut off wing the same as leg. Slanting the knife in slightly may make it easier to hit the joint. Lift the wing onto another plate.

3 Slice the white meat, starting at tip of breastbone and cutting down to wing joint. Carve enough for everyone, then cut meat from the leg and thigh. Need seconds? Turn platter; start over again.

Dutch-Oven Turkey

Practical platter: Handy two-pound frozen roast, macaroni, and vegetables.
Makes 6 servings

1 packaged frozen boneless turkey roast, (about 2 pounds)
2 tablespoons vegetable oil
½ teaspoon monosodium glutamate
½ teaspoon seasoned salt
¼ teaspoon seasoned pepper
1 envelope instant beef broth
   OR: 1 beef bouillon cube
1 medium-size onion, chopped
1 cup water
1 can (1 pound) cut green beans
2 cups thinly sliced celery
1 cup uncooked elbow macaroni

1 Remove turkey roast from foil package. Brown slowly in vegetable oil in a Dutch oven or electric skillet.
2 Stir in monosodium glutamate, seasoned salt and pepper, beef broth or bouillon cube, onion, and water. Heat to boiling; cover.
3 Simmer, turning meat once or twice, 2 hours, or until tender. Remove to a cutting board; keep warm while cooking vegetables and macaroni.
4 Pour liquid from Dutch oven into a 4-cup measure; drain liquid from green beans into same cup. Add water, if needed, to make 4 cups. Return to Dutch oven; heat to boiling.
5 Stir in celery, macaroni, and beans. Cook, stirring several times, 10 minutes, or until macaroni and celery are tender and almost all of the liquid has evaporated. Spoon vegetables onto a heated large deep platter.
6 Carve turkey into ¼-inch-thick slices; arrange, overlapping, over vegetables. Sprinkle lightly with chopped parsley, if you wish.

●

Turkey Roast Royale

Roast at 350° about 2½ hours. Makes 8 servings, plus enough for a bonus meal

1 frozen boneless white-and-dark-meat turkey roast (about 4½ pounds)
¼ teaspoon seasoned salt
¼ teaspoon pepper
3 tablespoons butter or margarine
1 cup dry white wine
2 tablespoons flour
¼ cup water
   Apricot Stuffing (recipe follows)

1 Thaw turkey roast, following label directions; remove from wrapper or carton. Place roast, skin-side up, on a rack in a small roasting pan; sprinkle with salt and pepper. Insert meat thermometer into roast so bulb reaches center.
2 Melt butter or margarine in a small saucepan; stir in wine. Pour over roast; cover.
3 Roast in moderate oven (350°), spooning liquid in pan over roast several times, 1½ hours; uncover.
4 Continue roasting 1 hour, or until thermometer registers 185° and roast is lightly browned. Remove roast from pan; keep warm while making gravy.
5 Pour liquid from pan into a 1-cup measure; add water or dry white wine, if needed, to make 1 cup. Return to pan; heat to boiling.
6 Smooth flour and the ¼ cup water to a paste in a cup; stir into boiling liquid. Cook, stirring constantly, until gravy thickens and boils 1 minute. Season with salt and pepper, if needed.
7 Place roast on a heated large serving platter; spoon Apricot Stuffing around edge. Garnish

How to carve turkey making slices across the breast.

with canned apricot halves stuffed with pecans, and parsley, if you wish. Slice roast, removing strings as you go; serve gravy separately.

●

Apricot Stuffing
Bake at 350° for 1 hour. Makes 8 servings

    1 cup dried apricots, chopped
    1½ cups water
    1 cup diced celery
    ½ cup (1 stick) butter or margarine
    1 envelope instant chicken broth or 1 tea-
       spoon granulated chicken bouillon
    1 cup chopped pecans
    1 teaspoon salt
    12 slices white bread, toasted and cut in tiny
       cubes (6 cups)

1 Heat apricots and ½ cup of the water to boiling in a small saucepan; remove from heat. Let stand about 10 minutes.
2 Sauté celery in butter or margarine until soft in a medium-size frying pan; stir in remaining 1 cup water, chicken broth, pecans, and salt. Heat to boiling.
3 Place bread cubes in a large bowl; spoon apricot and celery mixtures over top; toss lightly until evenly moist. Spoon into an 8-cup baking dish; cover.
4 Bake in moderate oven (350°) 1 hour.

Turkey Platter Indienne
Buy one of the new about-two-pound boneless turkey roasts to cook, slice, and glaze for this easy curry-style dinner.
Roast at 400° for 2 hours, then bake at 350° for 15 minutes. Makes 8 servings

176

    1 packaged frozen boneless turkey roast
       (about 2 pounds)
    ½ cup apricot preserves (from a 12-ounce jar)
    ¼ cup apple cider
    1 teaspoon curry powder
       Herbed Pilaf (recipe follows)
       Sweet-potato Crispies (recipe follows)
       Golden Spiced Peaches (recipe follows)
       Sautéed Cucumber Wedges (recipe follows)
       Chopped radishes and green onions

1 Roast frozen turkey in its foil package, following label directions; remove from package; cool. (Meat slices more neatly if allowed to cool first.

Or roast turkey a day ahead and keep chilled until ready to finish dish.)
2 Cut turkey into 24 thin slices; place in a single layer in a jelly-roll pan, 15x10x1.
3 Mix apricot preserves, cider, and curry powder in a small saucepan; heat, stirring constantly, until preserves melt and sauce is hot; brush over turkey slices.
4 Bake in moderate oven (350°) 15 minutes, or until turkey is heated through and richly glazed.
5 Spoon *Herbed Pilaf* onto a large serving platter, mounding it in center; arrange turkey slices, overlapping, in a ring on top. Garnish with a preserved kumquat flower, if you wish. (To make, cut a preserved kumquat into eighths from tip almost to stem end; separate petals slightly; stuff with a sprig of parsley.)
6 Serve with little bowls of *Sweet-Potato Crispies, Golden Spiced Peaches, Sautéed Cucumber Wedges,* and chopped radishes and green onions to sprinkle on top.

●

Herbed Pilaf
Pan-toasted rice and bulgur wheat make this delectable go-with for curried turkey.
Makes 8 servings

    1 cup uncooked regular rice
    ¼ cup peanut oil or vegetable oil
    1 large onion, chopped
    1 cup chopped celery
    4 envelopes instant chicken broth
       OR: 4 chicken bouillon cubes
    1 teaspoon leaf rosemary, crumbled
    4 cups water
    1 cup bulgur wheat or wheat pilaf (from a 1-
       pound package)

1 Sauté rice, stirring constantly, in peanut oil or vegetable oil until toasty-golden in a large frying pan; remove with a slotted spoon and set aside. Stir onion and celery into drippings in pan; sauté just until soft.
2 Stir in chicken broth or bouillon cubes, rosemary, and water; heat to boiling, crushing cubes, if using, with a spoon. Stir in bulgur wheat and browned rice; cover.
3 Simmer, stirring once or twice, 1 hour, or until liquid is absorbed and wheat and rice are fluffy-tender.

●

Sweet-Potato Crispies
Just a few sprinkled over the turkey and pilaf add a pleasingly crunchy contrast.
Makes 8 servings

Frozen boneless turkey roasts are as easy to slice as a loaf of bread. Shown here, Turkey Roast Royale.

BIRDS OF A FEATHER

2 large sweet potatoes
Shortening or vegetable oil for frying

1 Pare sweet potatoes, then shred finely; pat dry on paper toweling.
2 Melt enough shortening or pour in enough vegetable oil to make a 2-inch depth in a small saucepan; heat to 350°.
3 Fry shredded potatoes, a heaping table-spoonful at a time, 1 to 2 minutes or until crisp. Lift out with a slotted spoon; drain well on paper toweling. Serve warm.

Golden Spiced Peaches
Jiffy-quick to fix and so good with turkey.
Makes 8 servings

1 can (1 pound) cling peach slices
1 tablespoon mixed pickling spices

1 Drain syrup from peaches into a small sauce-pan; stir in pickling spices. Heat to boiling, then simmer 5 minutes.
2 While syrup heats, cut each peach slice into thirds; place in a small bowl.
3 Strain syrup over peaches; cover; chill several hours to blend flavors.

Sautéed Cucumber Wedges
This popular vegetable is heated just long enough to take on a buttery-rich coating.
Makes 8 servings

2 large cucumbers
2 tablespoons butter or margarine

1 Pare cucumbers; quarter each lengthwise, then cut into ½-inch wedges.
2 Sauté in butter or margarine just until hot in a medium-size frying pan. Serve warm.

Drumstick Dinner
Bake at 375° for 40 minutes. Makes 4 servings

4 frozen turkey drumsticks, (about 1 pound each), thawed
2 tablespoons vegetable oil
1 large onion, chopped
1 teaspoon salt
¼ teaspoon pepper
1 can (about 14 ounces) chicken broth
½ cup ginger marmalade (from a 12-ounce jar)
⅓ cup light molasses
⅓ cup cider vinegar
⅓ cup prepared mustard
1 teaspoon ground ginger
Tangerine Risotto (recipe follows)

1 Brown drumsticks slowly in vegetable oil in a large frying pan; remove from pan.
2 Stir onion into drippings; sauté until soft. Stir in salt, pepper, and chicken broth; heat to boil-ing. Place drumsticks in sauce; cover. Simmer, turning several times, 1½ hours, or until tender. Remove drumsticks from pan and place on a rack in a shallow baking pan.
3 Blend marmalade, molasses, vinegar, mus-tard, and ginger in a small saucepan; heat slowly to boiling. Brush part over drumsticks.
4 Bake in moderate oven (375°), turning and brushing several times with remaining molasses mixture, 40 minutes, or until richly glazed.
5 Spoon *Tangerine Risotto* onto a heated large serving platter; arrange turkey drumsticks, spoke fashion, on top. Garnish platter with parsley and small cubes of jellied cranberry sauce, if you wish.

Tangerine Risotto
Makes 4 servings

1 cup uncooked regular rice
4 tablespoons (½ stick) butter or margarine
1 medium-size seedless orange
1 large onion, chopped
⅓ cup thawed frozen concentrated tangerine juice
1 can (5 ounces) water chestnuts, drained and sliced
1 teaspoon sugar
½ teaspoon salt

1 Cook rice in a large saucepan, following label directions. Stir in 2 tablespoons of the butter or margarine; keep warm.
2 While rice cooks, pare orange; section over a small bowl to catch the juice; cut each section in half.
3 Sauté onion in remaining 2 tablespoons but-ter or margarine until soft in a medium-size frying pan; stir in orange sections and juice, concentrated tangerine juice, water chestnuts, sugar, and salt. Heat slowly to boiling.
4 Pour over rice mixture; toss lightly to mix.

Deep Dish Turkey Pie
It's biscuit-topped, with chunks of turkey and vegetables in a savory sauce.
Bake at 425° for 30 minutes. Makes 6 servings

6 medium-size potatoes, pared and quartered
6 medium-size carrots, scraped and quartered
1 small onion, chopped
¼ cup chopped green pepper
2 tablespoons butter or margarine
1 can (10½ ounces) condensed cream
   of chicken soup
3 cups cooked turkey chunks
   Biscuit-Wedge Topping (recipe follows)

1 Cook potatoes and carrots in boiling salted water in large saucepan 15 to 20 minutes, or until tender; drain, saving 1 cup of liquid for next step.
2 While vegetables cook, sauté onion and green pepper in butter or margarine until soft in saucepan; stir in chicken soup and 1 cup saved liquid.
3 Spoon vegetables and turkey into 8-cup casserole: pour sauce over.
4 Bake in hot oven (425°) 15 minutes while making Biscuit-Wedge Topping; arrange biscuits on top of hot mixture; bake 15 minutes longer, or until biscuits are golden.
   BISCUIT-WEDGE TOPPING—Sift 1½ cups sifted all-purpose flour, 2 teaspoons baking powder, and ½ teaspoon salt into medium-size bowl; cut in ¼ cup (½ stick) butter or margarine; add ½ cup milk all at once; stir just until blended. Turn dough out onto lightly floured pastry cloth or board; knead lightly ½ minute; roll out to a 7-inch round; cut into 6 wedges; brush tops lightly with milk; sprinkle with ¼ teaspoon poppy seeds.

Turkey Alfredo

Cheese-seasoned noodles, breaded and browned slices of cooked turkey, and a rich saucy topping make this Continental treat.
Makes 4 servings

1 package (8 ounces) regular noodles
1 cup freshly grated Parmesan cheese
½ cup (1 stick) butter or margarine
   Supreme Sauce (recipe follows)
1 egg
1 teaspoon leaf oregano, crumbled
½ teaspoon salt
   Dash of pepper
2 tablespoons water
¾ cup fine dry bread crumbs
8 slices roast breast of turkey
3 tablespoons olive oil or vegetable oil

1 Cook noodles in a kettle, following label directions; drain; return to kettle. Add Parmesan cheese and 5 tablespoons of the butter or margarine; toss lightly with two forks until butter or margarine melts and noodles are evenly

coated. Keep hot. (Remaining butter or margarine is for Step 4.)
2 While noodles cook, make Supreme Sauce; set aside for Step 5.
3 Beat egg with oregano, salt, pepper, and water in a pie plate; place bread crumbs in a second pie plate.
4 Dip turkey slices into egg mixture, then into bread crumbs to coat well. Brown slices, a few at a time, in the remaining 3 tablespoons butter or margarine mixed with olive oil or vegetable oil in a large frying pan.
5 Spoon hot noodles into an 8-cup shallow broilerproof dish; arrange turkey slices, overlapping, on top; spoon Supreme Sauce over middle of turkey slices.
6 Broil, 4 inches from heat, 5 minutes, or until sauce puffs and turns golden.

Supreme Sauce

Whipped cream folded into the sauce adds the gourmet touch.
Makes about ¾ cup

2 tablespoons butter or margarine
2 tablespoons flour
1 envelope instant chicken broth
   OR: 1 chicken bouillon cube
½ cup milk
¼ cup cream for whipping

1 Melt butter or margarine in a small saucepan; stir in flour and chicken broth or bouillon cube. Cook, stirring constantly and crushing cube, if using, with a spoon, just until bubbly.
2 Stir in milk; continue cooking and stirring until sauce thickens and boils 1 minute; remove from heat.
3 Beat cream until stiff in a small bowl; fold into sauce.

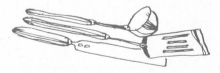

Turkey Tetrazzini

Bake at 350° for 1 hour. Makes 6 servings

1 package (8 ounces) thin spaghetti
4 tablespoons (½ stick) butter or margarine
4 tablespoons flour
¼ teaspoon salt
2 cups milk
1 can (3 or 4 ounces) sliced mushrooms
2 cups diced cooked turkey
1 can (4 ounces) pimientos, diced
2 tablespoons grated Parmesan cheese

179

1 Cook spaghetti, following label directions; drain. Place in a buttered 8-cup casserole.
2 While spaghetti cooks, melt butter or margarine over low heat in a medium-size saucepan. Blend in flour and salt; cook, stirring all the time, just until mixture bubbles. Stir in milk slowly, then liquid from mushrooms, plus enough water to make 1 cup; continue cooking and stirring until sauce thickens and boils 1 minute.
3 Stir in mushrooms, turkey, and pimientos; spoon over spaghetti; sprinkle with cheese.
4 Bake uncovered in moderate oven [350°] about 1 hour.

DUCKLING

Roast Duckling
It's smart planning to buy an extra bird just to have on hand to turn into a delectable second-day treat.
Roast at 325° about 3 hours. Makes enough for 2 meals, 6 servings each

3 frozen ready-to-cook ducklings (about 4½ pounds each), thawed
2 teaspoons salt
¼ teaspoon pepper
3 small onions, peeled and quartered
  Duck Giblet Broth (recipe follows)
  Golden Gravy (recipe follows)
  Pumpernickel Stuffing (recipe follows)

1 Wash and dry ducklings. Pierce skin all over with fork so fat will cook out. (Set giblets aside to simmer for broth.)
2 Rub skin with mixture of salt and pepper; stuff 4 onion quarters into cavity of each bird; place on rack in large roasting pan. (Or use two small pans, if necessary.)
180
3 Roast, uncovered, in slow oven (325°) 3 hours, or until drumstick joints move easily and ducklings are a rich golden-brown. (During roasting, pierce skin with fork several times. Also, to keep fat from smoking, dip it from roasting pan into a bowl several times during cooking. There will be as much as 6 cupfuls.)
4 Cut 2 ducklings into quarters. (Poultry shears do a fast job.) Arrange on heated serving platter. Serve with *Golden Gravy* and *Pumpernickel Stuffing*. (Set other duckling aside to cool.)
5 Wrap cooled duckling; chill with 4 cups of *Duck Giblet Broth* for *Duck Pilaf* for another meal.

Duck Giblet Broth
Combine giblets (except liver) and necks with 1 medium-size onion, chopped; handful of celery tops; 2 teaspoons salt; and 6 cups water in large saucepan. Simmer 1 hour, or until tender. Add livers for last 20 minutes' cooking. Strain stock; measure; add water, if needed, to make 6 cups. Save 4 cups for making *Duck Pilaf*. Grind or chop giblets fine and add to remaining 2 cups broth for *Golden Gravy*. Makes 6 cups.

Golden Gravy
Remove rack from roasting pan. Tip pan and pour off all fat into a bowl. Return 4 tablespoons to pan; blend in 4 tablespoons flour; cook, stirring all the time, just until mixture bubbles. Stir in 2 cups broth with ground giblets; continue cooking and stirring, scraping baked-on juices from bottom and sides of pan, until gravy thickens and boils 1 minute. Season to taste with salt and pepper. Makes about 2½ cups.

Pumpernickel Stuffing
Just peppery enough to go with juicy roast duck. Bake at 325° for 1 hour. Makes 6 servings

3 medium-size onions, chopped (1½ cups)
4 tablespoons drippings from ducklings
3 cups slightly dry pumpernickel-bread cubes (6 slices)
3 cups slightly dry white bread cubes (6 slices)
½ cup water
1 teaspoon salt
¼ teaspoon pepper

1 Sauté onions in drippings just until soft in large frying pan. Add bread cubes, water, salt, and pepper; toss lightly to mix. Spoon into 6-cup baking dish.
2 Bake with ducklings in slow oven (325°) 1 hour, or until crisp on top.

●

From Roast Duckling: Duck Pilaf
Sauté rice first to give it a toasty flavor, then blend with duckling and apricots to make this gourmetlike casserole.
Bake at 350° for 1½ hours. Makes 6 servings

1 roasted duckling
1 cup uncooked regular rice
3 tablespoons vegetable oil
1 cup chopped celery

A bird often overlooked is duckling; it's moderately priced though it looks *rich and regal when roasted.*

4 cups broth (from Duck Giblet Broth)
1 teaspoon salt
¼ teaspoon pepper
½ cup cut-up dried apricots

1 Remove skin from duckling; strip meat from frame, then dice. (There should be 3 cups.) Set aside for Step 4.
2 Sauté rice in vegetable oil in large frying pan, stirring often, just until golden; add celery and sauté 5 minutes longer.
3 Stir in broth, salt, and pepper; heat to boiling.
4 Spoon into 8-cup baking dish; stir in duckling and apricots; cover.
5 Bake in moderate oven (350°) 1½ hours, or until rice is tender and liquid is absorbed.

Roast Ducklings Halakahiki

Roast at 325° for 2½ hours. Makes 8 servings

2 ready-to-cook ducklings (about 5 pounds each)
2 teaspoons salt
2 tablespoons lemon juice
9 slices white bread, toasted and cubed
1 cup sliced green onions
2 cloves of garlic, sliced
½ teaspoon ground ginger
2 cans (3 or 4 ounces each) chopped mushrooms, drained
1 can (1 pound, 14 ounces) sliced pineapple
¾ cup (1½ sticks) butter or margarine, melted
¼ cup soy sauce
¼ cup honey
Mint
Mandarin Sauce (recipe follows)

1 Wash ducklings inside and out with cold water; dry well. Sprinkle salt and lemon juice into cavities. Smooth neck skin over back, then twist wing tips until they rest flat against sides.
2 Combine bread cubes, green onions, garlic, ginger, and mushrooms in a large bowl.
3 Drain syrup from pineapple into a small bowl and set aside for sauce. Dice 4 slices of the pineapple and add to bread mixture. Drizzle ½ cup of the melted butter or margarine over top; toss lightly to mix.
4 Spoon into cavities in ducklings, packing in lightly. Lace openings together with poultry pins or skewers and string. Place ducklings on a rack in a shallow roasting pan. Do not add any water or cover pan.
5 Roast in slow oven (325°) 1½ hours; pour all drippings from pan.
6 Combine remaining ¼ cup melted butter or margarine with soy sauce and honey in a small saucepan; heat, stirring constantly, to boiling. Brush part over ducklings.

7 Continue roasting, brushing with remaining soy mixture every 15 minutes, 1 hour, or until a drumstick moves easily and ducklings are richly golden.
8 Remove ducklings to a heated large serving platter. Garnish with remaining pineapple slices cut in half and mint.
9 Carve ducklings into quarters or cut with kitchen scissors; serve with *Mandarin Sauce*.

MANDARIN SAUCE—Mix 2 tablespoons cornstarch, ½ teaspoon ground ginger, and 2 envelopes instant chicken broth or 2 teaspoons granulated chicken bouillon in a small saucepan. Drain syrup from 1 can (about 11 ounces) mandarin orange segments into a 2-cup measure; add pineapple syrup and water, if needed, to make 2 cups; stir into cornstarch mixture. Cook, stirring constantly, until sauce thickens and boils 3 minutes; remove from heat. Fold in orange segments. Serve warm. Makes about 2½ cups.

Roast Duckling Jubilee

Three birds glazed sparkly-brown and arranged atop gourmetlike rice make a showy platter.
Roast at 325° for 3 hours. Makes 12 servings

3 ready-to-cook ducklings (about 4 pounds each)
1 teaspoon salt
3 small onions, peeled and quartered
1 medium-size apple, quartered, cored, and cubed
1 can (1 pound) whole figs
1 can (1 pound) dark sweet cherries
1 can (6 ounces) frozen concentrated orange juice, thawed
Pecan Pilaf (recipe follows)
3 preserved kumquats
Jubilee Sauce (recipe follows)

1 Wash ducklings inside and out with cold water; dry well. Pierce skin all over with a fork so fat will cook out.
2 Sprinkle cavity of each bird with part of the salt; stuff with onion quarters and apple cubes. Place ducklings, side by side, on a rack in a large roasting pan. (Or use two smaller pans, if necessary.)
3 Roast, uncovered, in slow oven (325°) 2½ hours.
4 While ducklings cook, drain syrups from figs and cherries into separate cups. Measure out ¼ cup of the fig syrup and 2 tablespoons of

Ducklings, like chicken, turkey and game hen, come fresh-frozen and can be enjoyed around the calendar.

the cherry syrup and mix with ¼ cup of the concentrated orange juice in a small bowl. (Set fruits and remaining syrups and orange juice aside for garnish in Step 7 and *Jubilee Sauce*.)

5 Brush ducklings with part of the orange mixture. Continue roasting, brushing several times with more orange mixture, 30 minutes, or until a drumstick joint moves easily and ducklings are richly golden. (During roasting, pierce skin several times with a fork and, to keep fat from smoking, remove from pan with a baster or dip out with a spoon.)

6 Spoon *Pecan Pilaf* onto a heated large serving platter; arrange ducklings on top.

7 Thread 3 figs and 2 cherries, alternately, onto each of 3 long kebab sticks; top each with a preserved kumquat; place around ducklings on platter.

8 Carve ducklings into quarters or cut with kitchen scissors; serve with *Jubilee Sauce*.

JUBILEE SAUCE—Mix 2 tablespoons cornstarch, ½ teaspoon salt, ¼ teaspoon dry mustard, and a dash of allspice in a medium-size saucepan. Blend in 1 cup water, ½ cup of the remaining concentrated orange juice, and ½ cup of the fig syrup. Cook, stirring constantly, until sauce thickens and boils 3 minutes. Stir in 2 tablespoons butter or margarine until melted, then remaining cherries and 2 teaspoons Worcestershire sauce; heat just until bubbly. Makes about 3 cups.

Hostess Note—Sauce may be made several hours ahead and reheated slowly until bubbly hot just before serving.

Pecan Pilaf

Cook the rice a day ahead, so each grain will be fluffy-dry and separate before frying.
Makes 12 servings

      6 *cups water*
      3 *envelopes instant chicken broth*
        OR: 3 chicken bouillon cubes
      3 *cups uncooked regular rice*
      1 *large onion, chopped*
      ½ *cup vegetable oil*
    1½ *teaspoons salt*
      ¼ *teaspoon mace*
      1 *cup chopped pecans*

1 Heat water with chicken broth or bouillon cubes to boiling in a kettle; stir in rice; cover. Cook 20 minutes, or just until rice is tender and liquid is absorbed.
2 Spoon into a large shallow pan; cool, then chill, for rice should be very dry, with each grain separate, before frying. (This should be done a day ahead.)
3 When ready to finish dish, sauté onion in 2 tablespoons of the vegetable oil until soft in a large frying pan; remove with a slotted spoon and place in a kettle. Add 2 more tablespoons of the vegetable oil to frying pan.
4 Fluff rice with a fork to separate grains; stir

one third into frying pan. Sauté, stirring gently several times, until lightly golden; remove and place in kettle. Repeat with remaining rice, half at a time, and vegetable oil; return all rice mixture to pan.
5 Stir in salt, mace, and pecans; cover. Heat slowly 8 minutes, or until hot.

Hostess note—Rice may be sautéed several hours before serving. Cover pan and keep at room temperature. Just before serving, reheat *very slowly*, allowing 15 to 20 minutes.

Roast Duck Orientale

In Chinese fashion the meat steams moist and tender from the inside as it roasts crispy brown outside.
Roast at 500° for 30 minutes, then at 325° for 1 hour. Makes 4 servings

      1 *ready-to-cook duckling (about 4 pounds)*
      2 *tablespoons soy sauce*
      1 *tablespoon sugar*
      1 *tablespoon pumpkin-pie spice*
      1 *teaspoon anise seeds*
      ½ *teaspoon ground ginger*
      1 *cup boiling water*
      4 *cups shredded romaine*

1 Wash duckling inside and out under running cold water; dry well. Skewer neck skin to back of bird; twist wing tips until they rest flat against skewered neck skin.
2 Mix soy sauce, sugar, pumpkin-pie spice, anise seeds, and ginger in a cup. Rub into skin and inside of duckling, then pour any remaining mixture into cavity. Place duck, breast down, on a plate; cover loosely; chill overnight.
3 When ready to roast duckling, mix any sauce on plate with boiling water; pour into body cavity, then close opening tightly with skewers.

184

Demonstrating the versatility of duckling: (left) Roast Ducklings Halakahiki in a glistening soy glaze and (right) classic roast duckling surrounded by orange baskets filled with cranberry sauce and applesauce.

Place duck, breast up, on a rack in roasting pan. Do not cover pan or add any water.

4 Roast in very hot oven (500°) 30 minutes; lower heat to slow (325°). Remove duckling from oven; dip all fat from pan with a spoon or baster, then return duckling to oven.

5 Continue roasting, spooning off fat as it cooks out, 1 hour, or until tender. (Drumstick should feel soft and twist and move easily.)

6 Place shredded romaine on a heated serving platter. Remove skewers from duckling, then set duckling on platter. Cut in four serving-size pieces with poultry shears, letting juices from cavity flow over romaine. Serve the duckling at once while the skin is at its crispiest, along with the romaine.

Pato De Natal
(Christmas Duck—Brazil)
Roast at 325° for 2½ hours. Makes 8 servings

    2 ready-to-cook ducklings (about 5 pounds each)
    1½ cups dry white wine
    ¼ cup lemon juice
    2 teaspoons salt
    1 clove of garlic, minced
    ¼ cup chopped parsley
    ¼ cup sliced green onions
    1 large onion, chopped
    4 tablespoons (½ stick) butter or margarine
    1 can (1 pound) chestnuts, drained and chopped
    ¼ teaspoon ground nutmeg
    ¼ teaspoon pepper
    3 cups small slightly dry bread cubes (6 slices)
    ¼ cup sifted all-purpose flour

1 Remove giblets from cavities of ducklings. Wash ducklings inside and out with cold water; dry well. Place in a large shallow dish. Chop giblets.
2 Mix wine, lemon juice, salt, garlic, parsley, and green onions in a small bowl; pour over ducklings. Let stand, turning several times, at least 4 hours at room temperature, or overnight in refrigerator, to season.
3 Sauté large onion in butter or margarine until soft in a large frying pan; stir in chopped giblets. Cook, stirring several times, 5 minutes. Stir in chestnuts, nutmeg, and pepper. Pour over bread cubes in a large bowl; toss lightly until evenly moist.
4 Remove ducklings from marinade; pat dry. Strain marinade into a 2-cup measure and set aside for making gravy. Stuff chestnut mixture into neck cavities of ducklings; smooth neck skin over back, then twist wing tips until they rest flat against back. Stuff body cavities; lace openings together with poultry pins or skewers and string. Place ducklings, breast up and side by side, on a rack in a large roasting pan. Do not cover pan.
5 Roast in slow oven (325°) 2½ hours, or until ducklings are tender and richly browned. (During roasting, prick skin several times with a fork and, to keep fat from smoking, remove from pan with a baster or dip out with a spoon.) Remove

ducklings to a heated large serving platter; keep warm while making gravy.
6 Pour all fat from roasting pan into a cup, then measure ¼ cupful and return to pan. Blend in flour; cook, stirring constantly, until bubbly. Add water to marinade to make 2 cups; stir into roasting pan. Continue cooking and stirring until gravy thickens and boils 1 minute.
7 Garnish ducklings with parsley and ruffled green-onion tops threaded through thin lemon slices, if you wish. Carve ducklings; serve gravy separately to spoon over meat and stuffing.

●

Twin Duck Barbecue
Use kitchen shears to cut each tender duck into serving-size quarters
Makes 8 servings

    2 frozen ready-to-cook ducklings (about 4½ pounds each), thawed
    6 cups water
      Handfull of celery tops
    1 small onion, sliced
    4 peppercorns
      Orange-spice Barbecue Sauce (recipe follows)

1 Pierce skin of ducklings all over with fork so fat will cook out.
2 Simmer, covered, in water with celery tops, onion, and peppercorns in large kettle 2 hours, or just until barely tender. Remove ducks and drain well. (This much can be done ahead.)
3 When ready to grill, place ducks on grill about 10 inches above hot coals; brush with *Orange-Spice Barbecue Sauce*. Grill, turning and basting often, 1½ hours, or until joints move easily and ducks are a rich golden brown.
4 Cut each into quarters for serving.

●

Orange-Spice Barbecue Sauce
It gives a golden-glaze goodness to grilled ducklings. Delicious with chicken, too
Makes 1½ cups

    ¼ cup sugar
    2 tablespoons cornstarch
    ½ teaspoon ground allspice
    ½ teaspoon ground cloves
    1 cup orange juice
    2 tablespoons vinegar
    4 tablespoons (½ stick) butter or margarine

Combine sugar, cornstarch, allspice, and cloves in small saucepan; stir in orange juice and vinegar. Cook, stirring constantly, until sauce thickens and boils 3 minutes. Stir in butter or margarine.

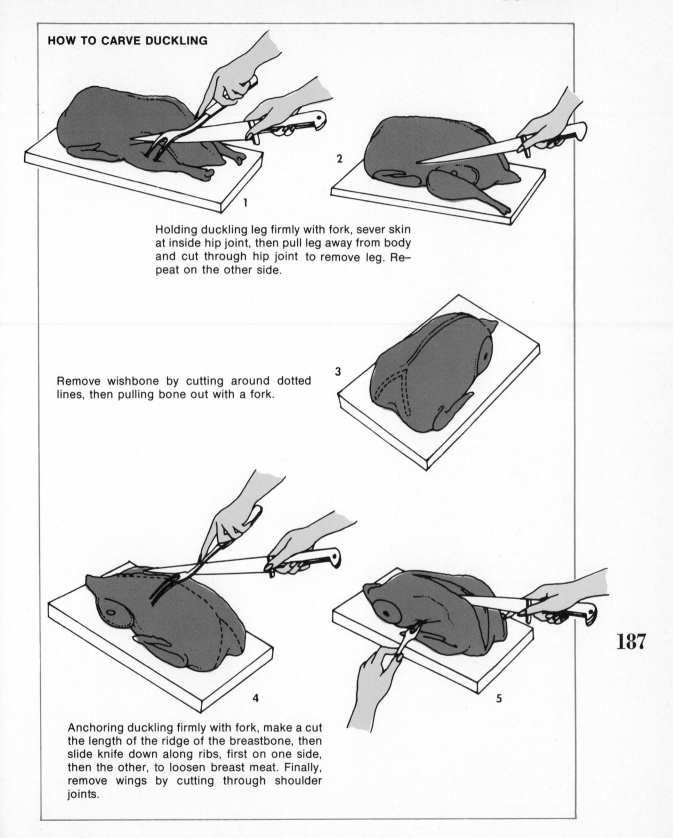

HOW TO CARVE DUCKLING

Holding duckling leg firmly with fork, sever skin at inside hip joint, then pull leg away from body and cut through hip joint to remove leg. Repeat on the other side.

Remove wishbone by cutting around dotted lines, then pulling bone out with a fork.

Anchoring duckling firmly with fork, make a cut the length of the ridge of the breastbone, then slide knife down along ribs, first on one side, then the other, to loosen breast meat. Finally, remove wings by cutting through shoulder joints.

187

GOOSE

Roast Goose with Fruit Stuffing
Roast at 325° for 3½ hours. Makes 6 servings

  1 *frozen young goose (about 9 pounds)*
  1 *package (11 ounces) mixed dried fruits*
  1 *cup orange juice*
10 *slices white bread, toasted and diced*
  ½ *teaspoon ground ginger*
  ½ *teaspoon ground cinnamon*
  ½ *teaspoon ground nutmeg*
  ¼ *teaspoon ground cloves*
    Apricot brandy
    Giblet Gravy (recipe follows)

1 Thaw goose 2 or 3 days in refrigerator. Remove giblets; also remove any large pieces of fat from inside goose. Rinse with cold water; drain.
2 Dice fruit; combine with orange juice in small bowl; let stand about 30 minutes.
3 Combine bread and spices in large bowl; pour fruit mixture over; toss until evenly moistened (mixture will seem somewhat dry).
4 Stuff about 1 cup fruit dressing in neck cavity; fold skin over and hold in place with wing tip or skewers.
5 Stuff remaining dressing into body cavity. Close vent with skewers or sew with needle and thread.
6 Place goose on rack in shallow pan; prick with two-tined fork in fatty areas around legs and wings. Do not cover; do not add water.
7 Roast in slow oven (325°) 1 hour; remove accumulated fat from pan. Drain fat twice more, roasting goose 3 hours in all. Brush goose with apricot brandy; roast 30 minutes longer, brushing with apricot brandy every 10 minutes. Remove to heated platter. To serve, carve breast into thin slices and separate drumsticks and thighs at joints. Garnish platter with chicory and red grapes, if you wish.

GIBLET GRAVY: Cook neck, gizzard, and heart in salted water in small saucepan (with celery tops, if you wish) 2 hours, or until tender; add liver; cook 15 minutes longer. Drain, adding water if needed to make 2 cups. Dice meat, discarding bone and gristle. Measure ¼ cup of drippings from roasting pan into medium-size saucepan; stir in ¼ cup of sifted all-purpose flour until blended. Stir in 2 cups broth; cook and stir until mixture thickens and boils 1 minute. Stir in diced meat and 1 tablespoon chopped parsley. Add salt and pepper to taste.

189

A Dickensian feast: roast goose stuffed with fruits.

BIRDS OF A FEATHER

Roast Watertown Goose
With Stewed Apples

Roast at 325° for about 4 hours. Makes 6 servings

1 frozen young goose (about 12 pounds),
  thawed
  Salt
4 cups water
½ onion, sliced
6 peppercorns
¼ pound butter
2 tablespoons flour
2 cups water
  Stewed Apples (recipe follows)

1 Wash goose inside and out; drain; pat dry.

2 Rub with salt inside and out. Close vent with skewers or sew with needle and thread. Fold neck skin over flat against back and hold in place with wing tip or skewers.

3 Place, breast up, in baking pan. Add water, onion, and peppercorns.

4 Roast in moderate oven (325°) F.), about 4 hours until leg joints move easily. When water has boiled down, baste frequently with butter which has been browned.

5 Remove goose to warmed platter. Place pan on top of range. Stir flour into fat. Add 2 cups water. Stir and let boil 2 or 3 minutes, until smooth and slightly thickened. Serve with goose.

Stewed Apples
Makes 6 servings

2 pounds apples
2 tablespoons butter
½ cup sugar
½ cup water
½ cup white wine
1 small piece lemon peel
1 tablespoon lemon juice

1 Wash apples; peel and core. Cut fruit in thick slices.
2 Sauté in butter 2 or 3 minutes. Sprinkle with sugar. Add water, wine, lemon peel, and lemon juice.
3 Cover; cook slowly until apples are tender.

ROCK CORNISH GAME HENS

Rock Cornish Game Hen Platter
Brown these little birds, then bake in an herb-wine sauce and serve with pilaf.
Bake at 350° for 1 hour. Makes 8 servings

      8 frozen Rock Cornish game hens (about 1 pound each), thawed
         Salt and pepper
   ¼ cup unsifted all-purpose flour
   5 tablespoons butter or margarine
   1 small onion, chopped
   1 can (about 14 ounces) chicken broth
   1½ cups dry white wine
   2 tablespoons chopped parsley
   1 bay leaf
   ½ teaspoon leaf basil, crumbled
   ½ teaspoon leaf thyme, crumbled
   2 tablespoons cornstarch
   ¼ cup cold water
      Mushroom Pilaf (recipe follows)
   1 can (about 1 pound, 14 ounces) peeled whole apricots, drained

   1 can (1 pound, 14 ounces) sliced pineapple, drained
      Sugared Grapes (recipe follows)

1 Rinse Cornish hens inside and out; pat dry. Sprinkle insides with salt and pepper; coat outsides lightly with flour. Brown, several at a time, in butter or margarine in a large frying pan; place in a large roasting pan.
2 Sauté onion until soft in drippings in same frying pan; stir in chicken broth, wine, parsley, bay leaf, basil, thyme, ½ teaspoon salt, and ¼ teaspoon pepper; pour into roasting pan; cover.
3 Bake in moderate oven (350°) 1 hour, or until hens are tender; lift out with a wide spatula and keep warm while making gravy.
4 Smooth cornstarch and water to a paste in

Cornish Hens Indienne, gorgeous little game hens seasoned inside with thyme, basted with a piquant curry glaze, arrive at the table nestling in a fluffy bed of Parsley Rice bracketed by carrots.

a cup; stir into liquid in roasting pan. Cook, stirring constantly, until gravy thickens and boils 3 minutes; remove bay leaf.

5 When ready to serve, spoon *Mushroom Pilaf* onto a large serving platter; arrange Cornish hens in a circle on top. Place an apricot on each pineapple slice and arrange around edge of platter; tuck *Sugared Grapes* around pineapple. Garnish pilaf with a bouquet of celery tops, if you wish.

SUGARED GRAPES—Wash small clusters of seedless green grapes; dry well. Beat 1 egg white with ½ teaspoon water in a small bowl. Dip grapes into egg mixture, then roll in granulated sugar on waxed paper to coat well. Let stand on paper toweling to dry.

Mushroom Pilaf

Toasting the rice first gives it a wonderfully gourmetlike flavor.
Makes 8 servings

½ *pound fresh mushrooms*
  OR: 2 *cans (3 or 4 ounces each) chopped mushrooms*
6 *tablespoons olive oil or vegetable oil*
2 *cups uncooked regular rice*
½ *cup toasted slivered almonds (from a 5-ounce can)*
2 *tablespoons chopped parsley*
1 *teaspoon salt*
3 *envelopes instant chicken broth*
  OR: 3 *chicken bouillon cubes*
5 *cups water*

1 Wash fresh mushrooms; trim; chop. Sauté lightly in 2 tablespoons of the olive oil or vegetable oil in a large frying pan; remove with a slotted spoon and set aside. (If using canned mushrooms, set aside for Step 3.)
2 Stir rice and remaining 4 tablespoons olive oil or vegetable oil into same pan; heat slowly, stirring constantly, until rice is toasty-golden.
3 Stir in mushrooms (or canned mushrooms and liquid), almonds, parsley, salt, chicken broth or bouillon cubes, and water. Heat to boiling, crushing bouillon cubes, if used, with a spoon; cover.
4 Simmer 25 minutes, or until rice is tender and liquid is absorbed. Fluff up with a fork before serving.

Golden-Crisp Rock Cornish Hens

Little birds in coats of seasoned crumbs bake invitingly brown with no turning, no watching. Bake at 350° for 1 hour and 15 minutes. Makes 6 servings

6 *frozen Rock Cornish game hens (about 1 pound each), thawed*
  Salt
½ *cup buttermilk*
2 *packages seasoned coating mix for chicken*
1 *package (1 pound) spinach noodles*
½ *teaspoon onion salt*
2 *tablespoons butter or margarine*

1 Remove giblets from Cornish hens and chill to simmer for gravy another day. Rinse hens inside and out; pat dry. Sprinkle cavities lightly with salt.
2 Brush hens, one at a time, with buttermilk, then shake in coating mix. Place, breast side up and not touching, in a jelly-roll pan.
3 Bake in moderate oven (350°) 1 hour and 15 minutes, or until tender and golden.
4 While hens bake, cook noodles in a kettle, following label directions; drain; return to kettle. Add onion salt and butter or margarine; toss lightly to mix.
5 Spoon noodles onto a large deep serving platter; arrange Cornish hens on top. Garnish with sprigs of water cress, if you wish.

●

East-West Broiled Cornish Hens

The flavor trick is, when broiling these little birds, to baste frequently with the marinade which keeps them especially moist.
Makes 6 servings

3 *frozen Rock Cornish game hens (about 1 pound each), thawed*
½ *cup soy sauce*
1½ *cups water*
2 *green onions, trimmed and chopped*
¼ *teaspoon crushed red pepper*
1 *small head romaine, shredded (about 4 cups)*
2 *tablespoons dry sherry*
  Chinese noodles

1 Cut hens in half with poultry shears or kitchen scissors. Place in a large shallow broiling pan, without rack.
2 Combine soy sauce, ½ cup of the water, green onions and red pepper; pour over hens. Marinate 1 hour.
3 Broil hens, 4 inches from heat, turning often and basting with marinade, 40 minutes, or until hens are a rich brown.

4 Line a heated serving platter with shredded romaine. Arrange hens on romaine; keep warm.
5 Stir remaining 1 cup water and sherry into broiling pan.
6 Cook, stirring and scraping cooked-on bits from sides of pan, until liquid comes to boiling. Spoon over hens. Serve with Chinese noodles.

●

Cornish Hens Indienne

Roast at 375° for 1 hour and 20 minutes. Makes 6 servings

6 frozen Rock Cornish game hens (about 1
  pound each), thawed
  Salt
¼ teaspoon pepper
¼ teaspoon leaf thyme, crumbled
½ cup (1 stick) butter or margarine, melted
4 slices bacon, diced
1 medium-size onion, chopped
1 tablespoon flour
1 tablespoon sugar
2 teaspoons curry powder
2 teaspoons instant chicken bouillon
1 cup apricot nectar
1 tablespoon lemon juice
  Parsley Rice (recipe follows)
  Buttered carrots

1 Remove giblets from body cavities of hens and save to simmer for soup. Rinse hens inside and out; pat dry with paper toweling.
2 Mix 1 teaspoon salt with pepper and thyme in a cup; sprinkle ¼ teaspoonful inside each hen; tie legs together. Place hens, breast side up, in a jelly-roll pan. Brush with part of the melted butter or margarine.
3 Roast in moderate oven (375°), brushing once or twice with remaining melted butter or margarine and drippings in pan, 1 hour. Cut away strings with scissors; spoon all drippings from pan.
4 While hens roast, sauté bacon until amost crisp in a medium-size saucepan; remove with a slotted spoon and drain on paper toweling. Stir onion into drippings; sauté until soft.
5 Blend in flour, sugar, curry powder, chicken bouillon, and ½ teaspoon salt; cook, stirring constantly, until bubbly. Stir in apricot nectar and lemon juice. Heat, stirring constantly, to boiling; simmer 5 minutes, or until mixture thickens slightly; spoon about half over hens.
6 Roast 10 minutes; spoon remaining curry mixture over top to make a thick coating. Continue roasting 10 minutes, or until hens are tender and richly glazed.
7 Spread *Parsley Rice* on a large deep serving platter; arrange hens on top. Spoon carrots at each end.

PARSLEY RICE—Combine 1 cup uncooked regular rice, 2 tablespoons butter or margarine, 2 teaspoons instant chicken bouillon, and 2¼ cups boiling water in a 6-cup baking dish; cover. Bake along with hens in moderate oven (375°) 1 hour, or until rice is tender and liquid is absorbed. Fluff rice with a fork; stir in ¼ cup chopped parsley. Makes 6 servings.

BREADS

BREADS—BACK TO BAKING YOUR OWN: YEAST BREADS, QUICK BREADS, PANCAKES AND WAFFLES, FRITTERS AND FRIED BREADS, COMMERCIAL BREADS

Sales of yeast are up, we're told, about 20 percent. And of flours, particularly such health-giving specialty flours as whole wheat and rye. Women today are following their grandmothers' lead and baking their own bread.

No culinary art gives greater satisfaction than baking one's own bread. What a joy it is to feel the "life" of yeast dough in the hands, for it *is* a living thing. And what a pleasure it is to see the loaves rise tall and handsome, to smell their yeasty goodness as they bake.

Quick breads are rewarding to make, too— perfect feathery muffins, for example, jeweled, perhaps, with raisins or blueberries . . . tender flaky biscuits or nut-rich golden corn breads . . . souflé-light pancakes . . . crisp brown waffles . . . too-good-to-be-true, old-fashioned yeast-raised doughnuts.

You'll find all the recipes here plus a good many more. Also, ingenious ways of jazzing up bread and biscuit mixes, commercial refrigerator rolls and store-bought loaves.

Two beautiful breads: rustic Sesame Twist and feathery, refined Golden Brioche (not for beginners).

YEAST BREADS

White Bread
(Rapid-mix method)
Golden brown slices just pull apart for easy serving.
Bake at 400° for 30 minutes. Makes two 21-ounce loaves

5½ cups sifted all-purpose flour
 1 envelope active dry yeast
 3 tablespoons sugar
 2 teaspoons salt
1½ cups water
 ½ cup milk
 3 tablespoons vegetable oil
 ¼ cup (½ stick) butter or margarine

195

1 Mix 2 cups of the flour, yeast, sugar and salt in a large bowl.
2 Heat water, milk and oil in a small saucepan until very warm to the touch (not scalding); add to flour. Beat with electric mixer at medium speed 2 minutes, scraping bowl several times.
3 Blend in ¾ cup more flour at low speed, then beat at high speed for 3 minutes. Stir in remaining flour to make a soft dough.
4 Turn out onto a lightly floured pastry board and knead until smooth and elastic, about 10 minutes, using only as much flour as needed

to keep dough from sticking. Place in a greased large bowl; turn to coat all over with shortening; cover with a clean towel. Let rise in a warm place, away from draft, for 1½ hours, or until it has doubled in bulk.

5 Punch dough down; turn out onto lightly floured pastry board; invert bowl over dough; allow to rest 10 minutes.

6 Divide dough in half and knead each half several times. Roll out each half to a 16x8-inch rectangle. Roll up firmly from short side, jelly-roll fashion. Cut roll into 12 slices. Brush each slice with melted butter or margarine; stack slices to reshape as loaf in a greased 8½x4½x2½-inch loaf pan. (Turn loaf pan on a short side and rest against back of counter for ease of stacking slices in pan.)

7 Let rise again in a warm place, away from draft, 1 hour, or until double in bulk.

8 Bake in hot oven (400°) 30 minutes, or until golden and loaves give a hollow sound when tapped. Remove from the pans to wire racks and then cool completely.

Sourdough Bread

Since the days of the gold rush in Alaska, people have been making a special type of bread that uses the yeast in the air as the leavening agent. The bread is called sourdough because of the particular flavor that the starter gives to the bread. Our method takes about 7 days to make, but once you have your starter made, measure the required amount for the recipe and replace with an equal amount of flour and milk. In the past, people had more time, so only the sourdough starter was used to raise the bread—it took 24 hours. To quicken the process we add commercial yeast, but you will still get that special flavor.

Bake at 400° for 40 minutes. Makes two 17-ounce loaves

    1 envelope active dry yeast
    1 cup very warm water
 1½ cups Sourdough Starter (recipe follows)
    2 tablespoons sugar
    2 teaspoons salt
 5½ cups sifted all-purpose flour
    1 egg white
    2 tablespoons cold water

1 Sprinkle yeast into very warm water in a large bowl. (Very warm water should feel comfortably warm when dropped on wrist.) Then stir in starter, sugar and salt.

2 Beat in 2 cups of the flour until smooth. Beat in enough of the remaining flour to make a soft dough.

3 Turn out onto lightly floured pastry board. Knead until smooth and elastic, about 10 minutes, using only as much flour as needed to keep dough from sticking.

4 Place in a greased large bowl, turn to coat all over with shortening; cover with a clean towel. Let rise in a warm place, away from draft, 1 hour, or until double in bulk.

5 Punch dough down; turn out onto board; invert bowl over dough; let rest 20 minutes.

6 Grease two large cooky sheets; sprinkle with cornmeal.

7 Divide dough in half and knead each half a few times. Roll up tightly from long side, jelly-

The perfect loaf of home-baked bread is tall, brown and rounded with a good even break along the side.

The texture of home-baked breads should be somewhat rougher and firmer than that of commercially baked breads. When cool, they slice neatly without "crumbing;" they also toast magnificently.

roll fashion; pinch long seam tightly to seal. Roll loaf gently back and forth with hands to taper ends. Place loaf diagonally on prepared cooky sheet.

8 Roll out second half of dough to a 28-inch strip and roll up, jelly-roll fashion, starting from a long side. Shape roll into a ring on second cooky sheet.

9 Let rise again in a warm place, away from draft, 45 minutes, or until double in bulk.

10 Make slits 2 inches apart on top of breads with a very sharp knife or razor blade. Beat egg white and cold water together in a small cup. Brush loaves.

11 Bake in hot oven (400°) 40 minutes, or until golden and loaves give a hollow sound when tapped. Remove from cooky sheets to wire racks; cool completely.

Sourdough Starter
Makes 4 cups of starter

2 cups milk
2 cups sifted all-purpose flour

Pour milk into a glass or ceramic bowl and cover

bowl with cheesecloth. Let stand in the outdoors for 1 day. Stir in flour and recover bowl with cheesecloth. Place outside for 2 days. Place bowl in a sunny spot indoors and allow to stand until mixture bubbles and starts to sour, about 2 days. Spoon into a quart jar with a screw cap and store in refrigerator at least 1 day before using. (If top of starter should start to dry out at any time during this process, stir in a little lukewarm water.) When you remove 1½ cups of sourdough starter, simply combine ¾ cup milk and ¾ cup flour and stir into jar. Cover jar with cheesecloth and place in sunny spot for 1 day. Remove cheesecloth; cover jar and return to refrigerator.

How to Knead and Shape Bread

The mouthwatering loaves in these pages are yeast breads—yeast being the leavening agent rather than the baking powder, soda, steam or air used in so-called quick breads. Yeast makes dough rise and gives bread its porous texture. It is actually a small plant that "grows" under the proper temperature conditions. Yeast feeds on the sugar and starch of the dough and forms gas which makes the dough rise. It also gives yeast breads their tantalizing aroma and flavor. One of the secrets of success in yeast baking is temperature. The correct temperature of the water used to dissolve the yeast, the temperature at which the dough rises and the baking temperature are all important. Study the techniques shown here for mixing, kneading and shaping.

3 Push the dough away from you with the heels of both hands. If the dough sticks to the board, have a metal spatula handy to scrape the board clean; then re-flour and continue on.

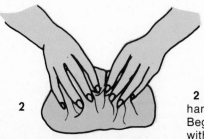

4 Give dough a quarter turn, then repeat folding, pushing, turning. As you knead, you will develop your own speed. You'll find well-kneaded bread dough is satiny, elastic and smooth.

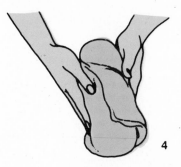

1 As a simple test for the "very warm" water that's needed to activate the yeast, hold the inside of your wrist under running water The water should feel comfortably warm when it's just right.

198

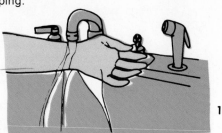

2 Turn soft dough out on floured board. Flour hands lightly, then pat dough to flatten slightly. Begin to knead this way: Pick up edge of dough with fingers and fold over toward you.

5 For an easy way to determine when dough has doubled in bulk: Press the dough flat in bowl, mark level, then remove dough. Fill bowl with water to double the first mark; mark level.

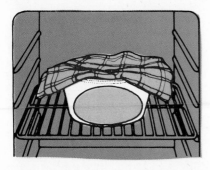

6 For warm, draft-free place to let dough rise, use oven with door closed. If the oven is electric, warm to 200°; then turn off and let cool for 5 minutes. If gas, pilot light will keep dough warm.

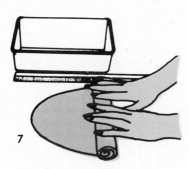

7 To shape a handsome loaf of bread: Roll or pat dough out to a rectangle with short side equal to length of a bread pan. Roll up the dough, in jelly-roll style, pressing the turns firmly.

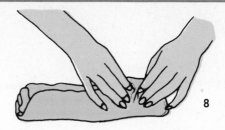

8 When loaf has been shaped, make sure dough is even on both ends. Then, with fingers, pinch long seam firmly—to seal and keep from unrolling. Put in pans, with seam on bottom.

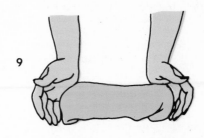

9 How to smooth ends of loaves: Press the dough down on each end of loaf with sides of hands. Tuck the thin strips formed under the loaf. Lift the loaf to the pan without stretching.

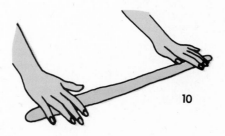

10 For shaping long loaves of bread: Roll up, in jelly-roll style, pinching seam, as in FIG. 8. Then, with the palms of your hands, taper the ends by rolling loaf back and forth on board.

199

Hi-Protein Bread
This special bread, higher in protein, is our version of the Cornell formula for increasing the nutritional value of bread.
Bake at 350° for 50 minutes. Makes two 26-ounce loaves

2 envelopes active dry yeast
2½ cups very warm water
1 cup nonfat dry milk
2 tablespoons honey
2 tablespoons vegetable oil
3 teaspoons salt

⅓ cup soya bean powder (from an
   11-ounce box)
2 tablespoons wheat germ
6½ cups sifted all-purpose flour

1 Sprinkle yeast into very warm water in a large bowl. (Very warm water should feel comfortably warm when dropped on wrist.) Stir until yeast dissolves, then stir in dry milk, honey, oil and salt.
2 Beat in soya bean powder and wheat germ with 2 cups of the flour until smooth. Beat in enough of the remaining flour to make a soft dough.
3 Turn out onto lightly floured pastry board. Knead until smooth and elastic, about 10 minutes, using only as much flour as needed to keep dough from sticking.
4 Place in a greased large bowl; turn to coat all over with shortening; cover with a clean towel. Let rise in a warm place, away from draft, 1 hour, or until double in bulk.
5 Punch dough down; turn out onto board; invert bowl over dough; allow to rest 20 minutes.
6 Divide dough in half and knead each piece a few times. Roll out each piece to an 18x9-inch rectangle. Roll up from short side, jelly-roll fashion. Press ends with hands to seal; fold under; place, seam side down, in a 9x5x3-inch greased loaf pan. Repeat with second half.
7 Let rise again in a warm place, away from draft, 40 minutes, or until double in bulk.
8 Bake in moderate oven (350°) 50 minutes, or until golden and loaves give a hollow sound when tapped. Remove from pans to wire racks; cool completely.

Cuban Bread

Crisp on the outside, even textured on the inside. Best to freeze the second loaf if you don't plan to serve it within two days.
Bake, starting in cold oven, 400° for 40 minutes.
Makes two 17½-ounce loaves

200

1 envelope active dry yeast
2 cups very warm water
2 tablespoons sugar
3 teaspoons salt
6 cups sifted all-purpose flour
   Ice water

1 Sprinkle yeast into very warm water in a large bowl. (Very warm water should feel comfortably warm when dropped on wrist.) Stir until yeast dissolves, then stir in sugar and salt.
2 Beat in 2 cups of the flour until smooth. Beat in enough of the remaining flour to make a soft dough.
3 Turn out onto a lightly floured pastry board.

Knead until smooth and elastic, about 5 minutes, using only as much flour as needed to keep dough from sticking.
4 Place in a greased large bowl, turn to coat all over with shortening; cover with a clean towel. Let rise in a warm place, away from draft, 1 hour, or until double in bulk.
5 Punch dough down; turn out onto board; invert bowl over dough; allow to rest 10 minutes.
6 Divide dough in half and knead each piece a few times. Roll out each piece to a 15x10-inch rectangle. Roll up tightly from long side, jelly-roll fashion; pinch long seam tightly to seal. Roll loaf gently back and forth to taper ends. Place loaf diagonally on a large cooky sheet which has been greased, then sprinkled with cornmeal.
7 Pat out second piece of dough to an 8-inch round and place on a second prepared cooky sheet.
8 Let rise again in a warm place, away from draft, 45 minutes, or until double in bulk.
9 Make slits 2 inches apart on top of loaves with a very sharp knife or razor blade; make crisscross slits, 2 inches apart, on round loaf. Brush all with ice water.
10 Place cooky sheets in cold oven.
11 Turn oven to hot (400°); bake 40 minutes, brushing several times with ice water, or until bread gives a hollow sound when tapped. Remove from cooky sheets to wire racks; cool completely.

Your Own French Bread

For your party, slice a whole loaf, then put back in its loaf shape on a serving board.
Bake at 450° for 15 minutes, then at 350° for 30 minutes. Makes 3 eighteen-inch-long loaves

1 envelope active dry yeast
2½ cups very warm water
7 cups sifted all-purpose flour
2 tablespoons sugar
1 tablespoon salt
   Corn meal
   Sesame seeds

1 Sprinkle into very warm water in large bowl. (Very warm water should feel comfortably warm when dropped on wrist.) Stir until yeast dissolves.
2 Stir in 2 cups of the flour and sugar and salt until mixture is smooth; gradually beat in enough of remaining 5 cups flour to make a stiff dough.
3 Turn out onto lightly floured pastry cloth or board; knead about 5 minutes, or until smooth

and elastic, adding only enough more flour to keep dough from sticking.

4 Return to bowl; brush top with soft shortening; cover with clean towel. Let rise in warm place, away from draft, 45 minutes, or until double in bulk.

5 Punch dough down; cover; let rise again 30 minutes, or until double in bulk.

6 While dough rises, make boat-shape baking pans this way: Tear off 3 twenty-inch-long sheets of heavy foil. Fold each in quarters lengthwise; grease; sprinkle lightly with corn meal. Pinch ends together and seal, pressing thumb inside to round slightly. Turn each side up to form an edge.

7 Punch dough down; knead 1 minute on lightly floured pastry cloth or board; divide in thirds. Roll out, one at a time, to a rope about 18 inches long; place in prepared foil pan.

8 Make several evenly spaced shallow cuts diagonally in top of each loaf; brush with water; sprinkle with sesame seeds. Cover; let rise in warm place, away from draft, 30 minutes, or until double in bulk.

9 Place pan of hot water on lower shelf in oven. Slide loaves on shelf above.

10 Bake in very hot oven (450°) 15 minutes; reduce heat to moderate (350°). Bake 30 minutes longer, or until bread gives a hollow sound when tapped. Remove immediately from pans; cool.

Sesame Twist
Bake at 375° for 45 minutes. Makes 1 large loaf

1¼ cups milk
  3 tablespoons honey
  2 tablespoons shortening
  2 teaspoons salt
  1 envelope active dry yeast
 ¼ cup very warm water
  4 cups sifted all-purpose flour
  1 egg, slightly beaten
  1 tablespoon sesame seeds

1 Scald milk with honey, shortening, and salt in a small saucepan; cool to lukewarm.

2 Sprinkle yeast into very warm water in a large bowl. (Very warm water should feel comfortably warm when dropped on wrist.) Stir until yeast dissolves, then stir in cooled milk mixture.

3 Beat in 2 cups of the flour to form a smooth soft dough. Gradually beat in remaining 2 cups flour to make a stiff dough.

4 Turn out onto a lightly floured pastry cloth or board; knead until smooth and elastic, adding only enough extra flour to keep dough from sticking.

5 Place in a greased large bowl; turn to coat

Off-beat breads to bake at home (clockwise from top): long Cuban Bread loaves, doughnut-shaped Sourdough, Hi-Protein Bread, sesame-studded Armenian Bread, Two-Tone Rye Twist, White Bread, Cuban Bread round.

201

all over with shortening; cover with a clean towel. Let rise in a warm place, away from draft, 1½ hours, or until double in bulk.

6 Punch dough down; knead a few times; divide in half. Divide one half into 3 equal-size pieces; roll each into a rope, 14 inches long. Braid ropes, pinching at ends to hold in place; place braid diagonally on a greased large cooky sheet or in a jelly-roll pan, 15x10x1.

7 Cut off one third of the second half of dough

and set aside for next step. Divide remaining into 3 equal-size pieces; roll each into a rope, 12 inches long, and braid, following Step 6; place on top of large braid on cooky sheet.

8 Repeat dividing into thirds, rolling, and braiding with remaining dough, making a braid about 10 inches long; place on top of other two braids; cover. Let rise again in a warm place, away from draft, 1 hour, or until double in bulk.

9 Brush loaf all over with slightly beaten egg; sprinkle with sesame seeds.

10 Bake in moderate oven (375°) 45 minutes, or until golden and loaf gives a hollow sound when tapped. (If loaf starts to get too brown after about 20 minutes' baking, cover top loosely with foil.) Remove from cooky sheet; cool on a wire rack.

Golden Brioche
Bake at 400° for 50 minutes. Makes one 9-inch loaf

½ cup milk
¾ cup (1½ sticks) butter or margarine
¼ cup sugar
1 teaspoon salt
1 envelope active dry yeast
¼ cup very warm water
4 eggs
4 cups sifted all-purpose flour

1 Scald milk in a small saucepan; cool to luke-warm.

2 Cream butter or margarine until fluffy-light in a large bowl; beat in sugar and salt.

3 Sprinkle yeast into very warm water in a cup. (Very warm water should feel comfortably warm when dropped on wrist.) Stir until yeast dissolves, then beat, a little at a time, into butter mixture; beat in milk until well-blended.

4 Beat eggs until creamy-thick in a small bowl; measure 2 tablespoonfuls into a cup; cover and chill for brushing loaf in Step 9. Beat remaining into butter mixture until well-blended.

5 Beat in flour, 1 cup at a time, until smooth, then continue beating 10 minutes. (Dough will be heavy and sticky.) Cover with a clean towel. Let rise in a warm place, away from draft, 2 hours, or until double in bulk.

6 Stir dough down; cover again; chill overnight.

7 When ready to shape, stir dough down again; turn out onto a very lightly floured pastry cloth or board; shape into an oval about 8 inches long. Cut off slightly less than ¼ of the dough and set aside to make the topknot.

8 Shape remaining dough into a smooth ball; place in a buttered 9-inch brioche pan or 8-cup round baking dish. Cut a deep 3-inch cross in center with a sharp knife; pull points upward and out with a knife to make a hollow for top.

9 Shape saved dough into a "pear;" place, narrow end down, in hollow in top of large ball. Tuck points in to make a smooth edge; cover. Let rise again, in a warm place, away from draft, 2 hours, or until double in bulk. Brush all over with saved beaten egg.

10 Bake in hot oven (400°) 50 minutes, until loaf is richly golden and gives a hollow sound when tapped. Remove from pan; cool on a wire rack.

Two-Tone Rye Twist
Light and dark rye, twisted together, start from the same basic dough.
Bake at 350° for 45 minutes. Makes two 20-ounce loaves

4 cups sifted all-purpose flour
4 cups whole-rye flour
2 envelopes active dry yeast
2½ cups very warm water
¼ cup (½ stick) butter or margarine, melted
⅓ cup dark molasses
3 teaspoons salt
2 teaspoons caraway seeds, crushed
1 cup whole-bran cereal
¼ cup dry cocoa (not a mix)
2 teaspoons instant coffee
Corn meal
Butter or margarine, melted
1 teaspoon cornstarch
½ cup cold water

1 Combine 3 cups all-purpose flour with rye flour in a medium-size bowl; blend well; reserve.

2 Sprinkle yeast into very warm water in a large bowl. (Very warm water should feel comfortably warm when dropped on wrist.) Stir until yeast dissolves; stir in butter or margarine, molasses, salt and caraway. Pour one half of mixture into a second large bowl.

3 To one half of the yeast mixture, add the bran, cocoa and coffee, stirring to mix well. Stir in enough of the rye-flour mixture to make a soft dough (about 3 cups). Turn dough out onto a lightly floured pastry board. Knead until smooth and elastic, about 5 minutes, using only as much of the remaining all-purpose flour as needed to keep dough from sticking.

4 Place dough in a greased medium-size bowl; turn to coat all over with shortening; cover with clean towel. Let rise in a warm place, away from draft, 45 minutes, or until double in bulk.

5 To remaining half of yeast mixture, stir in enough rye-flour mixture, part at a time, to make a soft dough (about 3½ cups). Turn out onto lightly floured board. Knead until smooth and elastic about 5 minutes, adding only as much of the remaining all-purpose flour as needed to keep dough from sticking. Let rise as in Step 4.

6 Grease two large cooky sheets; sprinkle with cornmeal.

7 When both doughs have doubled, punch down; knead each a few times; divide each in half. Roll each of the four pieces on board with hands to form a thick rope 18 inches long. For each loaf: Twist light and dark rope together; pinch together at ends. Place loaf on cooky sheet; repeat with remaining 2 ropes.

8 Let rise again in a warm place away from draft, 45 minutes, or until double in bulk. Brush lightly with melted butter or margarine.

9 Bake in moderate oven (350°) 45 minutes, or until loaves give a hollow sound when tapped.

10 While loaves are baking, combine cornstarch with cold water in small saucepan; stir until smooth. Cook, stirring constantly, until mixture thickens and boils 1 minute. Brush over baked loaves; return to oven; bake another 3 minutes. Remove from cooky sheets to wire racks; cool completely.

Cheese Bread
Each slice of this mellow moist bread tastes teasingly of snappy Cheddar.
Bake at 350° for 45 minutes for medium-size loaves, 30 minutes for miniature ones. Makes 4 medium-size loaves, or 2 medium-size and 6 miniature loaves, or 12 miniature loaves

1 cup milk
2 tablespoons sugar
3 teaspoons salt
1 tablespoon butter or margarine
1 envelope active dry yeast
1 cup very warm water
5 cups sifted all-purpose flour
2 cups grated sharp Cheddar cheese (8 ounces)

1 Scald milk with sugar, salt, and butter or margarine in a small saucepan; cool to lukewarm.

2 Sprinkle yeast into very warm water in a large bowl. (Very warm water should feel comfortably warm when dropped on wrist.) Stir until yeast dissolves, then stir in cooled milk mixture.

3 Beat in 1 cup of the flour; sprinkle cheese

over and beat in until completely blended. Beat in remaining 4 cups flour gradually to make a stiff dough.

4 Turn out onto a lightly floured pastry cloth or board; knead until smooth and elastic, adding only enough extra flour to keep dough from sticking.

5 Place in a greased bowl; turn to coat all over with shortening; cover with a clean towel. Let rise in warm place, away from draft, 1 hour, or until double in bulk.

6 Punch dough down; knead a few times, then shape this way: If making all medium-size loaves, divide dough in quarters; shape each into a loaf. If making medium-size and miniature loaves, divide dough in half; shape one half into 2 loaves, then divide remaining half into sixths; shape each into a loaf. If making all miniature loaves, divide all the dough in twelfths; shape each into a loaf. Place medium-size loaves in greased pans, 7½x3¾x2¼; miniature ones in greased toy-size loaf pans; cover. Let rise again in warm place, away from draft, about 1 hour, or until double in bulk.

7 Bake in moderate oven (350°) 45 minutes for medium-size loaves, 30 minutes for miniature ones, or until bread gives a hollow sound when tapped. Remove from pans; brush tops with more butter or margarine; cool on wire racks. *Wrapping tip:* Cool bread completely, then wrap in transparent wrap. (Bread is likely to steam if wrapped warm.)

Anadama Cheese Bread
Perk up this old New England favorite with cheese and a bubble top.
Bake at 375° for 35 minutes. Makes two 28-ounce loaves

1½ cups water
½ cup corn meal
2 teaspoons salt
¼ cup vegetable shortening
½ cup light molasses
2 envelopes active dry yeast
½ cup very warm water
6 cups sifted all-purpose flour
8 ounces process American cheese, shredded (2 cups)
Butter or margarine, melted
Corn meal (for topping)

203

1 Combine 1½ cups water, ½ cup corn meal, salt, shortening and molasses in a medium-size saucepan. Heat, stirring constantly, until thick and bubbly. Pour into a large bowl; cool until lukewarm.

2 Sprinkle yeast into the ½ cup very warm water in a small bowl. (Very warm water should feel comfortably warm when dropped on wrist.) Stir until yeast dissolves; stir into corn meal mixture.

3 Beat in 2 cups of flour until smooth; stir in cheese, then about 3 more cups of the flour, one at a time, until mixture forms a soft dough.

4 Turn dough out onto lightly floured pastry board. Knead until smooth and elastic, about 8 minutes, using only as much flour as needed to keep dough from sticking.

5 Place in a greased large bowl; turn to coat all over with shortening; cover with a clean towel. Let rise in a warm place, away from draft, 45 minutes, or until double in bulk.

6 Punch dough down; knead a few times. Divide dough in half, then divide one half into 14 even-size balls, rolling each ball between palms of floured hands until surface is smooth. Place a row of 5 balls along each long side of a 9x5x3-inch greased loaf pan; place a row of 4 balls down the center. Repeat with remaining half of dough in a second loaf pan.

7 Brush tops of loaves with melted butter or margarine and sprinkle lightly with corn meal. Let rise in a warm place, away from draft, 30 minutes, or until double in bulk.

8 Bake in moderate oven (375°) 35 minutes, or until loaves give a hollow sound when tapped. Remove from pans to wire racks; cool completely. Loaves will break into separate rolls for serving.

Parmesan Garlic Bread

Brush pans with garlic butter to give just a tease of garlic flavor to the bread.
Bake at 400° for 40 minutes for large loaves, 30 to 35 minutes for small. Makes two 2-pound loaves, or 8 medium-size loaves, or 14 miniature-size loaves

2 cups milk
2 tablespoons sugar
2 teaspoons salt
2 envelopes active dry yeast
2 cups very warm water
10 cups sifted all-purpose flour
1 cup grated Parmesan cheese
2 tablespoons butter or margarine, melted
1 clove garlic, crushed
  Grated Parmesan cheese

1 Heat milk with sugar and salt in small saucepan just to lukewarm.

2 Sprinkle yeast into very warm water in a large bowl. (Very warm water should feel comfortably warm when dropped on wrist.) Stir until yeast dissolves, then stir in cooled milk mixture.

3 Beat in 5 cups flour and 1 cup cheese until completely blended. Beat in remaining flour gradually to make a soft dough.

4 Turn out onto lightly floured pastry board; knead until smooth and elastic, adding only enough extra flour to keep dough from sticking.

5 Place in greased large bowl; turn to coat all over with shortening; cover with a clean towel. Let rise in warm place, away from draft, 1 hour, or until double in bulk. Stir garlic into butter. Brush pans or casseroles with garlic butter.

6 Punch dough down; knead 1 minute on lightly floured pastry board, then shape this way: For large loaves, divide dough in half, divide each half in 7 even pieces, shape into rolls; place 6 rolls around edge of prepared pan and 1 in center. For medium-size loaves: Divide dough into 16 even pieces; shape into rolls, place 2 rolls in each of 8 prepared ten-ounce casseroles or custard cups. For miniature loaves: Divide dough into 14 pieces, shape into loaves, place in prepared toy-size loaf pans; cover. Let rise again in warm place, away from draft, 45 minutes, or until double in bulk. Brush tops with water; sprinkle lightly with extra Parmesan cheese.

7 Bake in very hot oven (400°) 40 minutes for large loaves, 30 to 40 minutes for small and medium loaves, or until breads give a hollow sound when tapped. Remove from pans to wire racks; cool completely.

Little Dill Cheese Loaves

Cottage cheese enhances the flavor of this simple-to-make batter bread.
Bake at 350° for 45 minutes. Makes 6 individual loaves

1 package active dry yeast
½ cup very warm water
1 cup (½ pound) cream-style cottage cheese
2 tablespoons sugar
1 tablespoon instant minced onion
2 teaspoons dill weed
1 teaspoon salt
¼ teaspoon baking soda
1 egg
2⅓ cups sifted all-purpose flour
  Butter or margarine

Clockwise from top: Vienna Crescent, Anadama Cheese Bread, Parmesan Garlic Bread, Taos Bread (in Vol. 1).

204

Fruit-studded Panettone is the traditional Christmas bread in Italy; its dough is sweet and soft. Similar sweet doughs can also be braided, then coiled. To make them brown, they're brushed with egg glaze.

1 Sprinkle yeast into very warm water in a large bowl. (Very warm water should feel comfortably warm when dropped on wrist.) Stir until yeast dissolves.

2 Heat cheese just until lukewarm in small saucepan; stir into yeast mixture; add sugar, onion, dill weed, salt, baking soda, egg and 1⅓ cups flour. Beat with electric mixer at medium speed for 2 minutes. Stir in the remaining flour to make a soft dough.

3 Cover with a clean towel. Let rise in a warm place, away from draft, 1 hour, or until double in bulk.

4 Stir dough down; spoon evenly into six 6-ounce soufflé dishes or custard cups.

5 Let rise again in warm place, away from draft, 45 minutes, or until double in bulk.

6 Bake in moderate oven (350°) 30 minutes; cover with foil, then bake 15 minutes longer, or until loaves give a hollow sound when tapped. Brush tops with butter or margarine; remove from dishes to wire racks. Serve warm or cool completely.

Vienna Crescent

This bread is made with the "sponge" method, which gives a fine texture inside and a lovely brown crust outside.

Bake at 450° for 10 minutes, then at 350° for

30 mintues for crescent, 40 minutes for loaf.
Makes 1 crescent and 1 loaf

2 envelopes active dry yeast
1 cup very warm water
4 teaspoons sugar
6 cups sifted all-purpose flour
1½ cups cold milk
3 teaspoons salt
1 egg, slightly beaten
Poppy seeds

1 Make "sponge": Sprinkle yeast into very warm water in a large bowl. (Very warm water should feel comfortably warm when dropped on wrist.) Stir until yeast dissolves.
2 Stir in 1 teaspoon sugar and 2 cups of the flour; beat until smooth. Cover bowl with plastic wrap or foil. Let rise in a warm place away from draft 2½ to 3 hours, or until large bubbles appear on the surface.
3 Stir in milk, remaining sugar, salt and 2 cups flour; beat until smooth; gradually add remaining flour. Turn out onto lightly floured pastry board; knead until smooth and elastic, about 5 minutes, using only as much flour as needed to keep dough from sticking.
4 Place in a greased large bowl; turn to coat all over with shortening; cover with clean towel. Let rise in warm place, away from draft, 1 hour, or until double in bulk.
5 Punch dough down; turn out onto board; knead 1 minute; divide in half. For crescent: Roll one half into a 30x24x24-inch triangle; roll up from long side to opposite point. Transfer to greased cooky sheet; shape into crescent. For loaf: Pinch off about 2 tablespoons dough from other half of dough and set aside for decoration; shape remaining dough into an 8-inch loaf. Place loaf on greased cooky sheet. With palms of hands, roll reserved dough into a 10-inch-long strip; place strip on top of loaf, folding it under at both ends. Cover; let rise again in a warm place, away from draft, 45 minutes, or until double in bulk.
6 Brush tops with slightly beaten egg; sprinkle with poppy seeds.
7 Bake in very hot oven (450°) 10 minutes, lower heat to 350° and bake 30 minutes longer for crescent and 35 to 40 minutes longer for loaf, or until breads give a hollow sound when tapped. Remove from cooky sheets to wire racks; cool completely.

2 envelopes active dry yeast
2¼ cups very warm water
¾ cup nonfat dry milk
3 tablespoons sugar
2 teaspoons salt
3 tablespoons olive or vegetable oil
6½ cups sifted all-purpose flour
¼ cup sesame seeds
1 egg, beaten

1 Sprinkle yeast into very warm water in a large bowl. (Very warm water should feel comfortably warm when dropped on wrist.) Stir until yeast dissolves, then stir in dry milk, sugar, salt and oil.
2 Beat in 2 cups of the flour until smooth. Beat in enough of the remaining flour to make a soft dough.
3 Turn out onto lightly floured pastry board. Knead until smooth and elastic, about 10 minutes, using only as much flour as needed to keep dough from sticking.
4 Invert a large bowl over dough and allow to rest 20 minutes.
5 Divide dough into 4 pieces. Divide one of these pieces into 3 pieces. Grease 3 cooky sheets with oil. Pat out one of the large pieces of dough to a 9-inch round on one of the cooky sheets. Make a 3-inch hole in center of round by pulling dough back with fingers. Pat a small piece of dough into a 3-inch round and place in center. Repeat to make 3 loaves. Cover each loaf with plastic wrap and chill 2 hours, or to a maximum of 6 hours.
6 Remove breads from refrigerator and remove plastic wrap. Allow to stand at room temperature 10 minutes.
7 Sprinkle sesame seeds on a shallow baking pan. Toast in a moderate oven (350°), 5 minutes, or just until golden.
8 Brush breads with beaten egg and sprinkle with toasted sesame seeds.
9 Bake in moderate oven (350°) 30 minutes, or until breads are golden and give a hollow sound when tapped. Remove from cooky sheets to wire racks; cool completely.

207

Armenian Bread
It looks like a flying saucer and is the perfect bread to serve at your next barbecue.
Bake at 350° for 30 minutes. Makes three 15-ounce rounds

Panettone
A traditional sweet fruit-filled bread from Italy. Delicious plain or toasted.
Bake at 375° for 1 hour and 15 minutes. Makes 1 large round loaf

½ cup milk
2 teaspoons anise seeds
½ cup sugar
1 teaspoon salt
1 envelope active dry yeast
¼ cup very warm water
2 eggs, beaten
2 teaspoons grated lemon rind
3 cups sifted all-purpose flour
½ cup (1 stick) butter or margarine, melted and cooled
1 jar (8 ounces) mixed candied fruits (1 cup), chopped fine
½ cup seedless raisins

1 Scald milk with anise seeds in small saucepan; remove from heat. Let stand 5 minutes, then strain into a cup, discarding seeds. Stir in ¼ cup sugar and salt. (Save remaining ¼ cup sugar for Step 6.) Cool just until warm.
2 Sprinkle yeast into very warm water in large bowl. (Very warm water should feel comfortably warm when dropped on wrist.) Stir until dissolved.
3 Stir in cooled milk mixture, eggs, lemon rind, and flour. Beat vigorously, scraping down side of bowl. Continue to beat with a spoon 100 times, or until dough is elastic and forms a ball. (This will take about 5 minutes.) Stir in cooled melted butter or margarine. Dough will become stringy, so beat again until it forms a ball.
4 Place in greased bowl; cover with clean towel. Let rise in warm place, away from draft, 1 hour, or until double in bulk.
5 While dough rises, prepare a 6-inch spring-form pan or 6-cup straight-side baking dish this way: Cut a piece of foil, long enough to wrap around pan and overlap slightly; fold in quarters lengthwise. Grease pan and foil strip, then wrap strip around top of pan to make a 2-inch stand-up collar; hold in place with paper clip and string.
6 Sprinkle saved ¼ cup sugar over raised dough; stir down; work in candied fruits and raisins. Place in pan.
7 Cover with clean towel; let rise in warm place, away from draft, 1½ hours, or until double in bulk.
8 Bake in moderate oven (375°) 1 hour and 15 minutes, or until a deep rich brown and loaf gives a hollow sound when tapped. Cool 5 minutes on wire rack. Remove foil collar, then remove bread from pan. Cool completely.

Old World Easter Bread
Idea for this towering sweet bread comes from Russia. If you don't have a tall mold, bake it in a deep bowl.
Bake at 350° for 40 minutes. Makes 1 loaf

⅓ cup milk
¼ cup sugar
½ teaspoon salt
4 tablespoons (½ stick) butter or margarine
1 envelope active dry yeast
¼ cup very warm water
1 egg, beaten
2 cups sifted all-purpose flour
¼ cup candied orange peel (from a 4-ounce jar)
¼ cup golden raisins
¼ teaspoon nutmeg
2 tablespoons fine dry bread crumbs
½ cup sifted 10X (confectioners' powdered) sugar
1 tablespoon water
Yellow food coloring

1 Scald milk with sugar, salt, and butter or margarine in small saucepan; cool just until warm.
2 Sprinkle yeast into very warm water in medium-size bowl. (Very warm water should feel comfortably warm when dropped on wrist.) Stir until yeast dissolves, then sitr in cooled milk mixture and egg.
3 Beat in 1 cup of the flour until smooth; stir in orange peel, raisins, and nutmeg; beat in remaining 1 cup flour to make a soft dough. Beat 100 times.
4 Coat top of dough lightly with butter or margarine; cover with clean towel. Let rise in warm place, away from draft, 1 hour, or until double in bulk.
5 Brush a 6-cup tall mold or 6-cup deep bowl with salad oil; sprinkle with bread crumbs. Punch dough down; beat 100 times. Spoon into mold.
6 Cover with clean towel; let rise in warm place, away from draft, 45 minutes, or until double in bulk.
7 Bake in moderate oven (350°) 40 minutes, or until loaf gives a hollow sound when tapped. Cool 5 minutes on wire rack; remove from mold or bowl.
8 Mix 10X sugar and water in a cup to make a thin frosting; drizzle half over loaf, letting it run down side. Blend a drop or two of yellow food coloring into remaining frosting to tint yellow; drizzle over loaf. Decorate top with a few slivered almonds, if you wish.

In the background, dripping with icing, Old World Easter Bread baked in a slim tall tower mold. In front of it, baked in both a round and a square pan, Walnut Stickies, gooey and caramely yeast rolls.

209

A new twist—Easter-Egg Ring with colorful Easter eggs baked right in. Just in front, Walnut Stickies baked in a big ring mold.

Easter-Egg Ring

A gay hot bread for Easter breakfast. The eggs hard-cook while the bread bakes.
Bake at 375° for 30 minutes. Makes 1 sixteen-inch ring

½ cup milk
2 tablespoons butter or margarine
¼ cup sugar
1 teaspoon salt
1 package active dry yeast
¼ cup very warm water
1 egg, beaten
3 cups sifted all-purpose flour
3 drops oil of anise
6 uncooked white-shell eggs
　Easter-egg coloring
　Butter or margarine

1 Scald milk with 2 tablespoons butter or margarine in small saucepan; stir in sugar and salt; cool to lukewarm.
2 Dissolve yeast in very warm water in large bowl. (Very warm water should feel comfortably warm when dropped on wrist.) Stir in cooled milk mixture and beaten egg.
3 Beat in 1 cup flour until smooth; beat in oil of anise. (Buy it at your drugstore.) Gradually beat in enough of remaining flour to make a stiff dough.
4 Turn out onto lightly floured pastry cloth or board; knead until smooth and elastic, adding only enough flour to keep dough from sticking.
5 Place dough in greased medium-size bowl; cover with clean towel; let rise in warm place, away from draft, 1 hour, or until double in bulk.
6 Tint uncooked eggs with Easter-egg coloring, following label directions; let dry while dough is rising.
7 Punch dough down; turn out onto lightly floured pastry cloth or board; divide into sixths. Roll each sixth into a rope, 12 inches long. Braid 3 ropes together on one side of a large cooky sheet; braid remaining ropes on other side. Form braids into one large circle, pinching ends together to make a tight seal.
8 Place each egg, large end up, in braid, spacing eggs evenly around ring. (The tiny air space in the large rounded end of the egg will keep it from cracking open during baking.) Cover with clean towel; let rise in warm place, away from draft, 1 hour, or until double in bulk.
9 Bake in moderate oven (375°) 30 minutes, or until golden-brown; brush top with butter or margarine; serve warm.

Basic Yeast Roll Dough

Bake at 400° for 15 minutes. Makes about 3 dozen rolls

1 envelope active dry yeast
¼ cup very warm water
⅓ cup butter, margarine or vegetable shortening
¼ cup sugar
1 tablespoon salt
2¼ cups scalded milk
1 egg, slightly beaten
7 to 8 cups sifted all-purpose flour

1 Crumble yeast into very warm water in a small bowl. (Very warm water should feel comfortably warm when dropped on wrist.) Stir until yeast dissolves.
2 Place butter, margarine or shortening, sugar and salt in a large mixing bowl; add scalded milk and stir until fat is melted and sugar and salt are dissolved. Let cool to lukewarm.
3 Stir yeast mixture into lukewarm milk mixture; add egg and beat until well mixed.
4 Add about half the flour and beat vigorously until smooth; beat in remaining flour, about ½ cup at a time, to make a soft dough.
5 Turn dough out onto a floured board, cover with turned-upside-down bowl and let rest 10 minutes; knead dough, adding only enough flour to keep it from sticking, about 10 minutes or until smooth and elastic.
6 Shape dough into a ball and place in a greased mixing bowl, turn to grease all over, cover with a clean towel and let rise in a warm place, away from draft, about 1 hour or until double in bulk.
7 Punch dough down, then shape into rolls, as desired, and place on greased baking sheets, cover rolls with clean towels; let rise again in a warm place, away from draft, about ½ hour or until double in bulk.
8 Bake in a hot oven (400°) 15 minutes or until golden. Brush tops lightly with butter or margarine, if you wish. Serve hot.

WAYS TO SHAPE YEAST ROLLS

PAN ROLLS: Divide dough into three equal parts and shape each into a fat sausage-like roll about 12 inches long. Slice each roll crosswise every 1 to 1½", roll slices into balls and place ¼" apart in greased 9-inch layer cake pans.

QUICKIE CLOVERLEAVES: Pinch off pieces of dough and roll into balls slightly larger than golf balls. Place in greased muffin-pan cups, then with kitchen shears, snip a cross into the top of each roll, forming "four-leaf clovers."

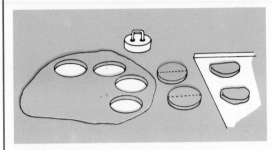

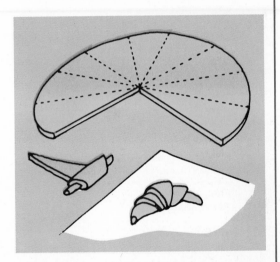

PARKER HOUSE ROLLS: Divide dough into three equal parts and roll, one at a time, on a floured board into a circle 9 inches across. Cut into rounds with a lightly floured 2½-inch biscuit cutter; brush each round with softened butter or margarine, make a crease across each slightly to one side of center, then fold larger "half" over smaller, forming half moons, and place on greased baking sheets one inch apart. Pinch edges lightly to seal.

BUTTERHORNS AND CRESCENTS: Divide dough into three equal parts and roll each on a floured board into a circle 12 inches in diameter and ¼" thick; spread with softened butter or margarine, then cut into 12 pie-shaped wedges. Beginning at the large end of each wedge, roll up and place, point down, on a greased baking sheet. To make CRESCENTS, simply bring ends of butterhorns in slightly.

CLOVERLEAF ROLLS: Divide dough into four equal parts, then working with one at a time, pinch off small pieces of dough and roll into balls about the size of marbles. Place three balls of dough in each cup of greased muffin pans, forming "three-leaf clovers."

211

Continued Page 212

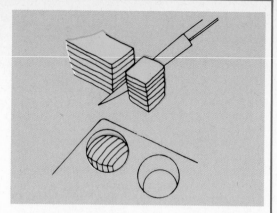

PINWHEELS: Divide dough into three equal parts and roll, one at a time, on a floured board into a rectangle 16 x 8 inches and about ¼ inch thick. Spread with softened butter or margarine and, if you like, cinnamon-sugar, jam or other filling. Roll up from the long side, jelly-roll style, then slice 1½ inches thick. Place pinwheels flat in greased muffin-pan cups.

FANTANS: Divide dough into three equal parts and roll each on a floured board into a rectangle 14 x 10 inches and about ¼ inch thick; cut crosswise into strips 1½ inches wide, then make a stack by piling 6 strips on top of one another. Cut stack crosswise into squares and place cut-sides down in greased muffin-pan cups.

Hot Cross Buns

These are Easter time's favorites of ''one-a-penny, two-a-penny'' fame.
Bake at 350° for 30 minutes. Makes 2 pans, 16 buns each

  2 *envelopes active dry yeast*
  ½ *cup very warm water*
  ½ *cup (1 stick) butter or margarine*
  ⅔ *cup evaporated milk*
  ½ *cup sugar*
  1 *teaspoon salt*
  2 *eggs*
  1 *cup dried currants*
4½ *cups sifted all-purpose flour*
  ¼ *teaspoon cinnamon*
  ¼ *teaspoon nutmeg*
    Lemon Icing (recipe follows)

1 Sprinkle yeast into very warm water in large bowl. (Very warm water should feel comfortably warm when dropped on wrist.) Stir until yeast dissolves.
2 Melt butter or margarine in small saucepan; remove from heat. Add evaporated milk, sugar, and salt, stirring until sugar dissolves; stir into yeast mixture.
3 Beat eggs in small bowl; measure 2 tablespoons into a cup and set aside for brushing buns in Step 8. Stir remaining into yeast mixture, then stir in currants.
4 Sift 2 cups of the flour, cinnamon, and nutmeg over yeast mixture; beat until smooth, then stir in just enough of remaining 2½ cups flour to make a soft dough.

5 Turn out onto lightly floured pastry cloth or board; knead until smooth and elastic, adding only enough flour to keep dough from sticking.
6 Place in greased bowl; brush top lightly with butter or margarine; cover with clean towel. Let rise in warm place, away from draft, 1 hour, or until double in bulk.
7 Punch dough down; turn out onto lightly floured pastry cloth or board; divide in half. Cut each half into 16 equal-size pieces; shape each lightly into a ball. Place each 16 balls in a greased baking pan. 9x9x2.
8 Cover with clean towel; let rise in warm place, away from draft, 45 minutes, or until double in bulk. Brush top of buns lightly with saved egg.
9 Bake in moderate oven (350°) 30 minutes, or until golden brown; remove from pans; cool on wire racks.
10 Drizzle LEMON ICING from tip of teaspoon on top of buns to make crosses.
  LEMON ICING—Blend 1 cup unsifted 10X (confectioners' powdered) sugar with 4 teaspoons milk, ¼ teaspoon vanilla, and ¼ teaspoon lemon extract until smooth in small bowl. Makes about ½ cup.

Almond Foldovers

Bake at 350° for 20 minutes. Makes 12 small loaves

  ¾ *cup milk*
  1 *cup sugar*

212

1 teaspoon salt
¾ cup (1½ sticks) butter or margarine
2 envelopes active dry yeast
¼ cup very warm water
2 eggs, beaten
5¼ cups sifted all-purpose flour
1½ cups golden raisins
1 container (8 ounces) candied red cherries, halved
1 teaspoon grated orange rind
1 can (8 ounces) almond paste
1 egg white, slightly beaten
10X (confectioners' powdered) sugar

1 Combine milk, ½ cup of the granulated sugar, salt, and ½ cup of the butter or margarine in a small saucepan. Heat slowly until butter or margarine melts; cool to lukewarm.

2 Sprinkle yeast into very warm water in a large bowl. (Very warm water should feel comfortably warm when dropped on wrist.) Stir until yeast dissolves, then stir in milk mixture and eggs.

3 Beat in 2 cups of the flour until smooth; stir in raisins, cherries, and orange rind. Beat in 3 cups more flour to make a stiff dough.

4 Turn out onto a lightly floured pastry cloth or board; knead until smooth and elastic, adding only enough of the remaining ¼ cup flour to keep dough from sticking.

5 Place in a greased large bowl; turn to coat all over with shortening; cover with a clean towel. Let rise in a warm place, away from draft, 2 hours, or until double in bulk.

6 While dough rises, crumble almond paste into a small bowl; stir in egg white and remaining ½ cup granulated sugar until smooth.

7 Punch dough down; knead a few times; divide into 12 even pieces. Pat each into an oval, 6x4, on a lightly floured pastry cloth or board; place, 2 inches apart, on greased large cooky sheets. Melt remaining ¼ cup butter or margarine in a small frying pan; brush part over ovals.

8 Divide almond mixture into 12 equal parts; with palms of hands, roll each into a 5-inch-long log. Place one lengthwise on half of each oval of dough; flatten slightly; fold dough in half. Press edges lightly to seal; cover. Let rise again, 1 hour, or until double in bulk. Brush with part of the remaining melted butter or margarine.

9 Bake in moderate oven (350°) 10 minutes;

Good at any time, but especially good at Easter, a huge pan of Hot Cross Buns, fresh from the oven.

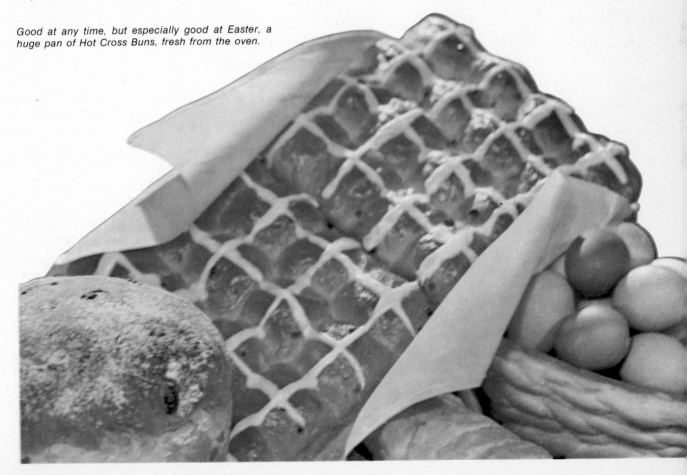

brush with remaining melted butter or margarine. Bake 10 minutes longer, or until golden, and loaves give a hollow sound when tapped. Remove from cooky sheets to wire racks; sprinkle with 10X sugar. Serve warm or cold.

Walnut Stickies

Bake them in rounds or squares.
Bake at 375° for 40 minutes. Makes 16 rolls

Dough

1 cup milk
¼ cup sugar
¾ teaspoon salt
2 tablespoons vegetable shortening
1 envelope active dry yeast
¼ cup very warm water
1 egg, beaten
2½ cups sifted all-purpose flour

Topping

¾ cup sugar
¾ cup water
1 teaspoon cinnamon
1 teaspoon grated orange rind
⅛ teaspoon salt
1 cup chopped walnuts

Filling

4 tablespoons (½ stick) butter or margarine, melted
¼ cup sugar
1 teaspoon cinnamon

1 Make dough: Scald milk with sugar, salt, and shortening in small saucepan; cool just until warm.
2 Sprinkle yeast into very warm water in large bowl. (Very warm water should feel comfortably warm when dropped on wrist.) Stir until yeast dissolves, then stir in cooled milk mixture. Beat in egg and 1½ cups of the flour until smooth; stir in remaining 1 cup flour to make a stiff dough.
3 Turn out onto lightly floured pastry cloth or board; knead until smooth and elastic, adding only enough flour to keep dough from sticking. Place in greased bowl; brush top lightly with shortening; cover with clean towel. Let rise in warm place, away from draft, 1 hour, or until double in bulk.
4 While dough rises, make topping: Combine sugar, water, cinnamon, orange rind, and salt in medium-size saucepan. Heat, stirring constantly, to boiling, then cook over medium heat 10 minutes, or until thick and syrupy. Pour half of the hot syrup into a greased baking pan,

214

8x8x2. (Or use a round 9-inch layer-cake pan.) Sprinkle evenly with walnuts. Set remaining syrup aside for glazing in Step 8.
5 To shape and fill rolls, punch dough down; turn out onto lightly floured pastry cloth or board. Roll out to a rectangle, 16x12. Spread generously with melted butter or margarine, then sprinkle with mixture of sugar and cinnamon.
6 Starting at long side of rectangle, roll up, jelly-roll style; cut crosswise into 16 slices. Place rolls, cut sides up, on nut-syrup mixture in pan.
7 Cover with clean towel; let rise in warm place, away from draft, 1 hour, or until double in bulk.
8 Bake in moderate oven (375°) 25 minutes. Remove from oven; spoon saved syrup over rolls. Bake 15 minutes longer, or until glazed and brown.
9 Cool in pan on wire rack 5 minutes; invert onto serving plate. Serve warm.

Basic Sweet Dough

¾ cup milk
¼ cup butter or margarine
⅓ cup sugar
1 teaspoon salt
¼ cup very warm water
2 packages active dry yeast
2 eggs, beaten
4½ to 5 cups sifted all-purpose flour

1 Scald milk in small saucepan; stir in butter or margarine, sugar, and salt; cool to lukewarm.
2 Measure very warm water into large bowl. (Very warm water should feel comfortably warm when dropped on wrist.) Sprinkle yeast into water; stir to dissolve; blend in milk mixture and eggs.
3 Stir in half the flour; beat until smooth; stir in enough of remaining flour to make soft dough, stirring until dough forms a ball that leaves side of bowl.
4 Turn out onto lightly floured pastry cloth or board; press into flat ball; knead until smooth and elastic, adding only enough flour to keep dough from sticking.
5 Place dough in greased large bowl; coat top lightly with soft shortening; cover; let rise in warm place, away from draft, about 50 minutes, or until double in bulk.
6 Punch dough down; turn out onto lightly floured pastry cloth or board; divide into thirds; shape and bake each third as desired (three suggestions follow).

Lemon Twist

Bake at 350° F. 20 to 25 minutes. Makes 1 braid

¾ cup sugar
1 tablespoon grated lemon rind
½ cup chopped walnuts
   Basic Sweet Dough (recipe precedes)
¼ cup melted butter or margarine (½ stick)
   Walnut halves

1 Combine sugar, rind, and nuts.
2 Roll ⅓ Basic Sweet Dough into rectangle, 10x16; spread with melted butter or margarine and sugar-nut mixture. Starting at long side of dough, roll up, jelly-roll fashion; press edge to seal; place on buttered cooky sheet.

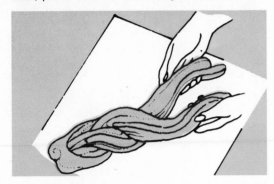

3 Cut lengthwise through middle to within 1 inch of one end; turn strips cut side up; twist strips around each other, keeping cut sides up, to form braid; seal ends.
4 Cover; let rise in warm place, away from draft, about 30 minutes, or until double in bulk; garnish with walnut halves.
5 Bake in moderate oven (350° F.) 20 to 25 minutes, or until golden-brown; place on wire cake rack to cool.

●

Glazed Cinnamon Twist
Bake at 350° F. 20 to 25 minutes. Makes 1 braid

   Basic Sweet Dough (recipe precedes)
½ cup melted butter or margarine (1 stick)
½ cup sugar
2 teaspoons cinnamon
½ cup sifted (10X confectioners' powdered) sugar
1½ teaspoons water

1 Roll ⅓ Basic Sweet Dough into rectangle, 10x16; spread with butter or margarine; sprinkle with sugar and cinnamon; fold one long side to center; fold other long side over, forming 3 layers; seal edges; place on buttered cooky sheet.
2 Cut lengthwise through middle to within 1 inch of one end; twist strips around each other to form braids; seal ends.

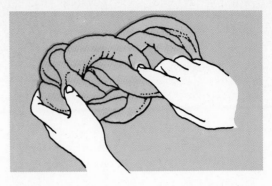

3 Make oval with braid; join ends; press firmly to seal; turn half of oval over to make a figure 8.
4 Cover; let rise in warm place, away from draft, about 30 minutes, or until double in bulk.
5 Bake in moderate oven (350° F.) 20 to 25 minutes, or until golden-brown; place on wire cake rack.
6 Blend 10X sugar and water; drizzle over warm braid.

●

Date-Nut Ring
Bake at 350° F. 20 to 25 minutes. Makes 1 ring

   Basic Sweet Dough (recipe precedes)
1 package (6½ ounces) pitted dates
½ cup sugar
½ cup water
½ cup chopped walnuts
¼ cup melted butter or margarine (½ stick)
   Sifted 10X (confectioners' powdered) sugar

1 While Basic Sweet Dough rises, combine dates, sugar, and water; bring to boiling; simmer 10 minutes, stirring constantly; remove from heat; stir in nuts; cool.
2 Roll ⅓ dough into rectangle, 10x16; spread with butter or margarine and date-nut mixture; fold one long side to center; fold other long side over, forming 3 layers; seal edges; place on buttered cooky sheet.
3 Cut lengthwise through middle to within 1

215

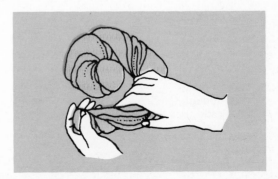

Two fabulous fruit breads, one quick (Polka-Dot Raisin Log, foreground), one not-so-quick (Candied Fruit Loaf, behind).

inch of one end; twist strips around each other to form braid; seal ends.

4 Starting with uncut end, wind braid around itself; tuck outer end under edge; press firmly to seal.

5 Cover; let rise in warm place, away from draft, about 30 minutes, or until double in bulk.

6 Bake in moderate oven (350° F.) 20 to 25 minutes, or until golden-brown; cool on cake rack; sift 10X sugar over top.

Candied Fruit Loaf

Bake at 350° for 35 minutes. Makes 2 large coffee cakes

5½ cups sifted all-purpose flour
  2 envelopes active dry yeast
  ⅓ cup sugar (for dough)
  2 teaspoons salt
  ¾ cup (1½ sticks) butter or margarine
  1 cup water
  ½ cup milk
  1 teaspoon vanilla
  2 eggs
  ¾ cup wheat germ
  1 cup mixed candied fruits, chopped
  2 tablespoons sugar (for filling)
  ½ cup finely chopped blanched almonds

1 Mix 2 cups of the flour, undissolved yeast, the ⅓ cup sugar, and salt in a large bowl; add ½ cup of the butter or margarine.

2 Heat water and milk until very warm to the touch (not scalding) in a small saucepan; add to flour mixture with vanilla. Beat with electric mixer at medium speed 2 minutes.

3 Beat eggs slightly in a small bowl; measure out 2 tablespoonfuls and set aside for glaze. Add remaining eggs and 1 cup more flour to yeast mixture; beat with electric mixer at high speed 1 minute, or until dough is thick and elastic. Stir in ½ cup of the wheat germ, candied fruits, and remaining flour to make a soft dough.

4 Turn out onto a lightly floured pastry cloth or board; knead until smooth and elastic, adding only enough extra flour to keep dough from sticking. Cover with transparent wrap; let stand 20 minutes.

5 Combine the 2 tablespoons sugar and remaining ¼ cup wheat germ in a small bowl; cut in remaining ¼ cup butter or margarine until mixture is crumbly; stir in almonds.

6 Divide dough in half; roll, half at a time, to a 12-inch square. Sprinkle half of the almond mixture over top; press in lightly; roll up, jelly-roll fashion. Place, seam side down, on a lightly greased cooky sheet. Repeat with second half of dough.

7 Make cuts, 1½ inches apart, along one side of roll from outer edge to center. Repeat on other side, spacing cuts halfway between those on opposite side. Turn each slice slightly on its side. Cover loosely with transparent wrap; chill 2 hours.

8 Remove from refrigerator; uncover; let stand 10 minutes. Stir 1 tablespoon water into remaining beaten egg; brush over coffee cakes.

9 Bake in moderate oven (350°) 35 minutes, or until golden and coffee cakes give a hollow sound when tapped. Remove from cooky sheets to wire racks; cool slightly. Garnish with small wedges of green and yellow candied pineapple, if you wish. Slice crosswise; serve warm or cold.

216

Carioca Pinwheel Loaf

Chocolate and spice go round and round in this brown-and-gold loaf.

Bake at 375° for 30 minutes. Makes 1 loaf

½ cup milk
4 tablespoons (½ stick) butter or margarine
¼ cup sugar
1 teaspoon salt
1 package active dry yeast
¼ cup very warm water
2 eggs, beaten
3 cups sifted all-purpose flour
1 square unsweetened chocolate, melted
½ teaspoon cinnamon
Syrup Glaze (recipe follows)

1 Scald milk with butter or margarine in small saucepan; stir in sugar and salt; cool to luke-
2 Dissolve yeast in very warm water in large bowl. (Very warm water should feel comfortably warm when dropped on wrist.) Stir in cooled milk mixture and beaten eggs.
3 Stir in 2 cups flour; beat until smooth. Gradually stir in enough of remaining flour to make a stiff dough.
4 Divide dough in half; turn out one half onto lightly floured pastry cloth or board. (Leave remaining half of dough in bowl for mixing with

chocolate and cinnamon in Step 6.) Knead until smooth and elastic, adding only enough flour to keep from sticking.
5 Place dough in greased medium-size bowl; cover with clean towel; let rise in warm place, away from draft, 1 hour, or until double in bulk.
6 Stir melted chocolate and cinnamon into remaining dough. (Do not worry if it is marbled, for chocolate will melt during baking.) Knead and let rise, as in Steps 4 and 5 above.
7 Punch both doughs down; roll out half of plain dough to ⅛-inch thickness on lightly floured pastry cloth or board. Cut into a rectangle. 10x8; lay on sheet of wax paper. Save dough cuttings for Step 9.
8 Roll out half of chocolate dough and cut the same as plain dough; place rectangle on top of plain dough; save cuttings for Step 9. Repeat Steps 7 and 8 with other halves of plain and chocolate doughs to make a total of 4 layers, ending with chocolate.
9 Roll chocolate cuttings into a rope, 8 inches long. Roll plain cuttings into a rectangle, 8x4; wrap around chocolate rope; place on one end of stacked layers. Roll up, as for jelly roll, starting at rope end.
10 Place, seam side down, in greased loaf pan, 9x5x3; make 4 shallow diagonal cuts in top of loaf. Cover with clean towel; let rise in warm place, away from draft, 1 hour, or until double in bulk.
11 Bake in moderate oven (375°) 30 minutes, or until loaf is golden-brown and gives a hollow sound when tapped; remove from pan. Brush with Syrup Glaze; cool on wire rack.

Syrup Glaze

Brush this sweet topping on coffeecakes while it's still warm.

Combine ½ cup light corn syrup and ¼ cup water in small heavy saucepan; heat slowly to a rolling boil; boil 1 minute. Store any remaining glaze in covered jar. Heat just before using. Makes ½ cup.

217

Two doughs of different flavors, one chocolate, one spice, twirled and baked together in one big loaf.

Turnover Fruit Bread

A homey fruit-filled loaf, fascinatingly inviting in its shapelessness.
Bake at 375° for 35 minutes. Makes 1 loaf

    1 package (13¾ ounces) hot-roll mix
    ¼ cup warm water
    4 tablespoons (½ stick) butter or margarine
    2 tablespoons sugar
    1 teaspoon grated lemon rind
    ¼ teaspoon salt
    2 eggs
      Fruit Filling (recipe follows)
      Butter or margarine
    2 tablespoons 10X (confectioners' powdered) sugar

1 Sprinkle yeast from hot-roll mix over warm water in 1-cup measure; stir to dissolve.
2 Cream 4 tablespoons butter or margarine with granulated sugar, lemon rind, and salt in medium-size bowl. Beat in eggs until mixture is light. Stir in dissolved yeast; blend in dry ingredients from hot-roll mix.
3 Turn out onto lightly floured pastry cloth or board; knead until smooth and elastic, adding only enough flour to keep dough from sticking. Place in greased bowl; cover with clean towel; let rise in warm place, away from draft, 1 hour, or until double in bulk.
4 Punch dough down; turn out onto lightly floured pastry cloth or board; roll out to a circle about ½ inch thick; turn over (so top will bake smooth); spread with *Fruit Filling* to within 1 inch of edge.
5 Pull edge of dough up and over all the way around to center to cover filling completely; pinch dough together to seal. Turn loaf over and place on cooky sheet. Cover with clean towel; let rise in warm place, away from draft, 1 hour, or until double in bulk.
6 Bake in moderate oven (375°) 35 minutes, or until golden-brown; brush top with butter or margarine; cool on wire rack. Sprinkle with 10X sugar.

FRUIT FILLING—Drain syrup from 1 can (about 9 ounces) crushed pineapple into small saucepan; add 1½ cups dried prunes. Cover; simmer 5 minutes; remove from heat and let stand 20 minutes, or until prunes are plump and syrup is absorbed. Pit prunes and cut in small pieces; stir in drained pineapple and 1 teaspoon pumpkin-pie spice, mixing well. Makes about 1½ cups.

218

Coffee Crown Cake

"Luscious" is the word for this handsome loaf, delicately flavored with orange and spice.
Bake at 350° for 30 minutes. Makes 1 nine-inch crown

    ¾ cup milk
    ⅓ cup sugar
    2 packages active dry yeast
    ½ cup very warm water
    2 eggs, beaten
    4 cups biscuit mix
    1 teaspoon ground cardamom
    ½ cup (4-ounce jar) candied orange peel
    ½ cup golden raisins
      Syrup Glaze (see recipe for Carioca Pinwheel Loaf)
    ½ cup 10X (confectioners' powdered) sugar
    1 tablespoon water

1 Scald milk in small saucepan; stir in sugar; cool to lukewarm.
2 Dissolve yeast in very warm water in large bowl. (Very warm water should feel comfortably warm when dropped on wrist.) Stir in cooled milk mixture and beaten eggs.
3 Beat in 2 cups biscuit mix and cardamom until smooth. Stir in orange peel and raisins, saving about 1 tablespoonful of each for decorating top, in Step 8. Beat in remaining biscuit mix to make a soft dough; then beat about 100 strokes to make bread high and light when baked.
4 Cover bowl with clean towel; let rise in warm place, away from draft, 1 hour, or until double in bulk.
5 Punch dough down; beat another 100 strokes; pour into well-greased 10-cup tube mold or 9-inch tube pan.
6 Cover with clean towel; let rise again in warm place, away from draft, 1 hour, or until double in bulk.
7 Bake in moderate oven (350°) 30 minutes, or until golden-brown. Cool in pan on wire rack 10 minutes; turn upside down and remove from pan. Brush with *Syrup Glaze*. let stand until cool.
8 Blend 10X sugar and water in cup; drizzle over crown; decorate with saved orange peel and raisins.

Almond Sugar Twist

Popular in Denmark, this sweet bread has an almond filling, a nut-sugar topping.
Bake at 375° for 30 minutes. Makes 1 large round loaf

    ¼ cup milk
    ½ cup (1 stick) butter or margarine
    ½ cup sugar
    ½ teaspoon salt
    1 envelope active dry yeast
    ¼ cup very warm water
    2 eggs
    3 cups sifted all-purpose flour
    ½ cup almond paste

3 tablespoons cold water
¼ cup sliced almonds

1 Scald milk in a small saucepan; stir in ¼ cup of the butter or margarine, ¼ cup of the sugar, and salt; cool to lukewarm.

2 Sprinkle yeast into very warm water in a large bowl. (Very warm water should feel comfortably warm when dropped on wrist.) Stir until yeast dissolves, then stir in cooled milk mixture.

3 Beat eggs in a small bowl; save 1 table-spoonful for Step 7; beat remaining into yeast mixture. stir in 2 cups of the flour until smooth; beat vigorously 100 strokes, then beat in remaining flour.

4 Place in a greased large bowl; cover with a clean towel. Let rise in a warm place, away from draft, 1¼ hours, or until double in bulk.

5 Mix almond paste with remaining ¼ cup butter or margarine, 3 tablespoons of remaining sugar, and 2 tablespoons of the cold water.

6 Punch dough down; knead until smooth and elastic on a lightly floured pastry cloth or board. Roll out to a rectangle, 20x10; spread with almond filling almost to edges. Starting at one long side, roll up, jelly-roll fashion. Place one end in the center of a greased large cooky sheet, then coil roll loosely round and round to make a "snail;" tuck end under. Cover; let rise again 30 minutes, or until double in bulk.

7 Stir remaining 1 tablespoon water into saved beaten egg; brush over "snail;" sprinkle with sliced almonds and remaining 1 tablespoon sugar.

8 Bake in moderate oven (375°) 30 minutes, or until golden and loaf gives a hollow sound when tapped. Remove from cooky sheet; cool on a wire rack. Serve warm or cold.

Shape Breads These Ways:

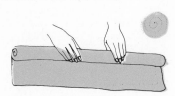

Almond Sugar Twist—Rolling dough, jelly-roll style, then winding, round and round, are the only tricks needed here. When making the coil, it's easy to handle if you place one end of roll on cooky sheet, then start winding.

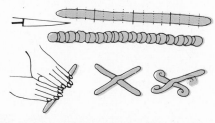

Saint Lucia Saffron Buns—Plain arithmetic keeps these little sweets even in size. First divide long roll of dough into quarters, then each quarter in fourths again. Roll pieces into 6-inch-long "pencils;" cross each two "pencils" as shown, then curve ends into neat coil

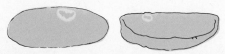

Stollen—This homey loaf starts with a big oval of dough folded over to resemble a jumbo Parker House roll.

Decorate Breads These Ways:

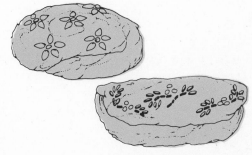

What could be simpler than sprinkling loaf with a snowy shower of 10X (confectioners' powdered) sugar? Yet it looks so festive! (Just press the sugar through a fine sieve right onto bread.) Or trim with sliced almonds (buy them in packages) arranged, petal fashion, around whole or halved candied cherries. Another flower idea: Cut stems and leaves from thin slices of candied citron or bright green gumdrops; use cherries for the blossoms.

219

Stollen

This traditional European fruit loaf looks like a giant Parker House roll.

Bake at 350° for 35 minutes. Makes 2 large loaves

1 cup seedless raisins
1 cup (8-ounce jar) mixed chopped candied fruits
¼ cup orange juice
¾ cup milk
½ cup sugar
1 teaspoon salt
1 cup (2 sticks) butter or margarine
2 envelopes active dry yeast
¼ cup very warm water
2 eggs, beaten
1 teaspoon grated lemon rind
5 cups sifted all-purpose flour
1 cup chopped blanched almonds
¼ teaspoon nutmeg
2 tablespoons cinnamon-sugar

1 Combine raisins, candied fruits, and orange juice in a small bowl.

2 Scald milk with sugar, salt, and ½ cup (1 stick) of the butter or margarine; cool to lukewarm. Sprinkle yeast into very warm water in a large bowl. (Very warm water should feel comfortably warm when dropped on wrist.) Stir until yeast dissolves, then stir in cooled milk mixture, eggs, and lemon rind.

3 Beat in 2 cups of the flour until smooth; stir in fruit mixture, almonds, and mutmeg, then beat in just enough of remaining 3 cups flour to make a stiff dough. Knead until smooth and elastic on a lightly floured pastry cloth or board, adding only enough flour to keep dough from sticking.

4 Place in a greased large bowl; cover with a clean towel. Let rise in a warm place, away from draft, 2 hours, or until double in bulk.

5 Punch dough down; knead a few times; divide in half. Roll each into an oval, 15x9; place on a greased large cooky sheet. Melt remaining ½ cup (1 stick) butter or margarine in a small saucepan; brush part over each oval; sprinkle with cinnamon-sugar; fold in half lengthwise. Cover; let rise again 1 hour, or until double in bulk. Brush again with part of the remaining melted butter or margarine.

6 Bake in moderate oven (350°) 35 minutes, or until golden and loaves give a hollow sound when tapped. While hot, brush with remaining melted butter or margarine; cool on wire racks.

●

Saint Lucia Saffron Buns

Sweden's famous Queen of Light festival inspired these dainty breakfast breads.

Bake at 400° for 12 minutes. Makes 32 buns

¼ cup milk
Pinch of saffron, crushed
¼ cup sugar
½ teaspoon salt
1 envelope active dry yeast
¼ cup very warm water
2 eggs
3 cups sifted all-purpose flour
½ cup (1 stick) butter or margarine, softened
Candied red and green cherries, cut in tiny squares
1 tablespoon cold water

1 Scald milk with saffron, sugar, and salt in a small saucepan; cool to lukewarm.

2 Sprinkle yeast into very warm water in a large bowl. (Very warm water should feel comfortably warm when dropped on wrist.) Stir until yeast dissolves, then stir in cooled milk mixture.

3 Beat eggs in a small bowl; save 1 tablespoonful for Step 5; beat remaining into yeast mixture. Stir in 1½ cups of the flour until smooth; beat in softened butter or margarine until completely blended, then beat in remaining flour to make a stiff dough. Knead until smooth and elastic on a lightly floured pastry cloth or board.

4 Place in a greased large bowl; cover with a clean towel. Let rise in a warm place, away from draft, 1 hour, or until double in bulk.

5 Punch dough down; knead several times; divide in quarters. Working with one at a time, roll into a rope; cut into 16 even-size pieces, then roll each into a 6-inch-long pencil-thin strip with hands. Cross each two strips on a greased large cooky sheet; curl each end into a small coil; decorate tip of each with a candied-cherry square. Repeat with remaining dough to make 32 buns. Cover; let rise again 30 minutes, or until double in bulk. Stir water into saved egg; brush over buns; sprinkle lightly with granulated sugar, if you wish.

6 Bake in hot oven (400°) 12 minutes, or until golden-brown. Remove from cooky sheet; cool on wire racks. Serve warm or cold.

Tips on Making Danish Pastry

Choose a cool day for your baking spree, for this buttery-rich dough handles best when it is cold. While rolling, if dough becomes too soft, place it as is in the refrigerator for 10 to 15 minutes. Another hint: If butter or margarine oozes out as you roll and fold dough, ease it back in, sprinkle the spot lightly with some flour from cloth, and continue.

Make the fillings you will need before making the dough. Some of the pastry recipes use all

Make your own Danish? Absolutely! The basic dough is here, also classic fillings and ways to shape.

of the filling, some a little less, so store whatever is left in a covered jar in the refrigerator. (Do not keep Vanilla-cream Filling longer than two days.)

Most of the pastry recipes call for the complete batch of dough. In those that use only half, a third, or less, suggestions are included for making the remainder into another treat.

To keep any of the dough, fold it into a block, place in a plastic bag or wrap in foil, transparent wrap, or wax paper, and store in the refrigerator. If not to be used the next day, it should be made into pastries and frozen.

To freeze pastries, shape and fill, and place on cooky sheets as for baking, then wrap sheets and all in foil or transparent wrap and freeze. Allow an additional 45 minutes of rising time when you take them from the freezer. Plan to use your frozen treats within 4 weeks.

●

Basic Danish Pastry
3 envelopes active dry yeast
½ cup very warm water
¾ cup milk
1 egg
⅓ cup sugar
1 teaspoon salt
4 cups sifted all-purpose flour
¾ pound (3 sticks) very cold butter or margarine

1 Sprinkle yeast into very warm water in a large bowl. (Very warm water should feel comfortably warm when dropped on wrist.) Stir until yeast dissolves, then stir in milk, egg, sugar, and salt.
2 Stir in 3¼ cups of the flour to make a soft dough. (Set remaining ¾ cup flour aside for next step.) Beat dough vigorously about 2 minutes, or 300 strokes, or until shiny and elastic.
3 Sprinkle pastry cloth or board with ⅔ of the remaining flour. Turn out dough; form into a flat ball; sprinkle with remaining flour. Roll out to a rectangle, 18x12.
4 Slice the *very cold* butter or margarine into thin strips lengthwise; place over ⅔ of the dough to form a 12-inch square.
5 Fold dough, brushing off excess flour each time, this way: Fold unbuttered third over middle third, then opposite end over top. Now fold into thirds crosswise to make a block, 6x4. It will

221

be 9 layers deep. Repeat rolling and folding as above 3 times more. (This gives the pastry its buttery-rich flakiness when baked.) Unless the dough gets too soft to handle easily, there is no need to chill it between the 3 rollings.
6 Now dough is ready to shape, fill, and bake, according to your choice of recipes.

Sugared Fans
They're simple to shape, yet so professional-looking. Fill with your choice of jams, or use our creamy cheese filling.
Preheat oven to 450°, Then lower heat to 375° and bake for 15 minutes. Makes 2 dozen

Roll out *Basic Danish Pastry* dough to a rectangle, 16x24, on a lightly floured pastry cloth or board. Cut lengthwise into quarters, then crosswise into sixths to make 24 four-inch squares. Place a generous tablespoonful of your choice of jam or *Cream-Cheese Filling (recipe follows)* across middle of each square; fold dough over and press edges together to seal. Cut about 4 slits, each ¾ inch long, in sealed edge; curve folded edge into a fan shape. Place, 4 inches apart, on greased cooky sheets. Cover; let rise in a warm place, away from draft, 1 hour, or until double in bulk. Brush tops with slightly beaten egg; sprinkle generously with sugar. Place in very hot oven (450°); lower heat to moderate (375°) at once. Bake 15 minutes, or until golden-brown.

Cheese Squares
Each square, folded envelope style, hides a cream-cheese filling.
Preheat oven to 450°, then lower heat to 375° and bake for 15 minutes. Makes 2 dozen

Roll out *Basic Danish Pastry* dough to a rectangle, 16x24, on a lightly floured pastry cloth or board. Cut lengthwise into quarters, then crosswise into sixths to make 24 four-inch squares. Place 1 tablespoonful *Cream-Cheese Filling (recipe follows)* in middle of each. Fold all 4 corners, overlapping slightly, to center to cover filling completely; press together to seal. (Edges will open during baking.) Place, 3 inches apart, on greased cooky sheets. Cover; let rise in a warm place, away from draft, 1 hour, or

until double in bulk. Brush tops with slightly beaten egg; sprinkle lightly with sugar. Place in very hot oven (450°); lower heat to moderate (375°) at once. Bake 15 minutes, or until golden-brown.

Cream-Cheese Filling
Combine 2 packages (8 ounces each) cream cheese, ¼ cup sugar, and 2 tablespoons lemon juice in a medium-size bowl; beat until blended. Makes about 2 cups.

Pinwheels
In Denmark, this classic has many fillings. Our choice is almond with strawberry jam.
Preheat oven to 450°, then lower heat to 375° and bake for 15 minutes. Makes 2 dozen

Roll out *Basic Danish Pastry* dough to a rectangle, 16x24, on a lightly floured pastry cloth or board. Cut lengthwise into quarters, then crosswise into sixths to make 24 four-inch squares. Starting at each corner, cut through pastry 1½ inches in toward center. Place 1 teaspoonful *Almond Filling (recipe follows)* in center of each square, then top with 1 teaspoonful strawberry jam. Pick up every other corner point and fold to center, overlapping points slightly and pinching together to hold, to make a pinwheel. Place, 4 inches apart, on greased cooky sheets. Cover; let rise in a warm place, away from draft, 1 hour, or until double in bulk. Brush tops with slightly beaten egg; sprinkle lightly with sugar. Place in very hot oven (450°); lower heat to moderate (375°) at once. Bake 15 minutes, or until golden-brown.

Almond Filling
Beat 1 egg white slightly in a small bowl. Stir in ½ cup almond paste (from an 8-ounce can) and ½ cup sugar. Mix lightly with a fork until well-blended. Makes about ⅔ cup.

Jam Foldovers
These easy-shape dainties have three fillings in one.
Preheat oven to 450°, then lower heat to 375° and bake for 15 minutes. Makes 2 dozen

Roll out *Basic Danish Pastry* dough to a rectangle, 16x24, on a lightly floured pastry cloth or board. Cut lengthwise into quarters, then crosswise into sixths to make 24 four-inch squares. Place 1 teaspoonful *Vanilla-Cream Filling (recipe follows)* in center of each and ½ teaspoonful each of raspberry and pineapple jams on either side. Fold one corner over filling to cover, then fold opposite corner over top. (Jams will show at either end and edges will open during baking.) Place, 4 inches apart, on greased cooky sheets. Cover; let rise in a warm place, away from draft, 1 hour, or until double in bulk. Brush tops with slightly beaten egg; sprinkle lightly with sugar. Place in very hot oven (450°); lower heat to moderate (375°) at once. Bake 15 minutes, or until golden-brown.

Vanilla-Cream Filling
Mix 2 tablespoons sugar and 2 tablespoons cornstarch in top of a small double boiler; stir in 1 egg yolk, then beat in 1 cup milk. Cook, stirring constantly, over simmering water 10 minutes, or until mixture thickens, then continue cooking, without stirring, 5 minutes longer. Pour into a small bowl; stir in 1 teaspoon vanilla; cool. Makes 1 cup.

Cream Buns
Leave this cream-filled treat plain or top with chocolate frosting.
Preheat oven to 450°, then lower heat to 375° and bake for 15 minutes. Makes 1 dozen

Divide *Basic Danish Pastry* dough in half; chill or freeze one half to make into more buns or *Danish Twists*, if you wish. Roll out the remaining half to a rectangle, 16x12, on a lightly floured pastry cloth or board. Cut lengthwise into quarters, then crosswise into thirds to make 12 four-inch squares. Place 1 tablespoonful *Vanilla-Cream Filling (recipe precedes)* in middle of each square. Fold the corners to center, pressing points and edges together to seal; place, folded side down, 4 inches apart, on greased cooky sheets. Cover; let rise in a warm place, away from draft, 1 hour, or until double in bulk. Brush tops with slightly beaten egg. Place in very hot oven (450°); lower heat to moderate (375°) at once. Bake 15 minutes, or until golden-brown. Serve plain, or cool and frost with *Chocolate Frosting (recipe follows)*.

Chocolate Frosting
Melt ½ cup semisweet-chocolate pieces (from a 6-ounce package) with 2 teaspoons short-ening, stirring often, until smooth in top of a small double boiler over simmering water. Makes enough for 12 *Cream Buns*.

Danish Twists
Each shattery-crisp butter-rich stick holds an almond filling.
Preheat oven to 450°, then lower heat to 375° and bake for 12 to 15 minutes. Makes 3 dozen

Divide *Basic Danish Pastry* dough in half; chill or freeze one half to make into more twists or *Cream Buns*, if you wish. Roll out the remaining half to a rectangle, 18x10, on a lightly floured pastry cloth or board; cut in half crosswise. Spread one half with about ½ cup *Almond Filling (recipe precedes);* top with second half, then cut in half crosswise to make two rectangles, each 9x5. Cut each crosswise into 18 one-half-inch-wide strips. Lift strips, 1 at a time, and twist carefully 3 or 4 times. Place, 3 inches apart, on greased cooky sheets. Cover; let rise in a warm place, away from draft, 1 hour, or until double in bulk. Brush tops with slightly beaten egg; sprinkle lightly with sugar. Place in very hot oven (450°); lower heat to moderate (375°) at once. Bake 12 to 15 minutes, or until golden-brown.

Whirligig Custard Cake
Rich cream-and-raisin filling goes between the base and pinwheel top of this beauty.
Preheat oven to 450°, then lower heat to 350° and bake for 40 minutes. Makes 1 eight-inch round cake

Divide *Basic Danish Pastry* dough into thirds; chill or freeze two thirds to make into more cakes or *Fruit-Cream Triangles*, if you wish. Roll out remaining third to a rectangle, 16x8, on a lightly floured pastry cloth or board; divide in half crosswise to make 2 eight-inch squares. Fit one square into the bottom of a greased 8-inch spring-form pan. (No need to cut dough into a circle as it is soft enough to shape easily.) Spread with ⅓ cup *Vanilla-Cream Filling (recipe precedes);* sprinkle with ¼ cup seedless raisins. Spread remaining 8-inch square with *Butter-Cream Filling (recipe follows)*. Roll up, jelly-roll fashion, then slice crosswise into 7 even-size rounds. Place, cut side up, on top of filling. Cover; let rise in a warm place, away from draft, 1 hour, or until double in bulk. Brush top with slightly beaten egg. Place in very hot oven (450°); lower heat to moderate (350°) at once. Bake 40 minutes, or until golden-brown. Cool 5 minutes on a wire rack; release spring and lift off side of pan, leaving cake on its metal

223

base. Serve plain or sprinkle with 10X (confectioners' powdered) sugar.

Butter-Cream Filling

Cream 4 tablespoons (½ stick) butter or margarine with ¼ cup sugar until fluffy in a small bowl; stir in ½ teaspoon almond extract. Makes ¼ cup.

Fruit-Cream Triangles

Just a third of the basic dough makes two open-face loaves to cut into triangles.
Preheat oven to 450°, then lower heat to 375° and bake for 25 minutes. Makes 2 loaves, or 20 triangles

Divide *Basic Danish Pastry* dough into thirds; chill or freeze two thirds to make into more triangles or *Whirligig Custard Cakes*, if you wish. Roll out the remaining third to a rectangle, 16x8, on a lightly floured pastry cloth or board; cut in half lengthwise to make 2 rectangles, each 16x4. Spread about 3 tablespoonfuls *Vanilla-Cream Filling* (recipe precedes) in a 1½-inch-wide band down middle, then spoon 4 tablespoonfuls *Prune Filling* (recipe follows) over top. Fold one long edge three quarters of the way over filling; overlap other edge over top about 1 inch. (Edges will open during baking.) Place loaves, 4 inches apart, on a greased cooky sheet. Cover; let rise in a warm place, away from draft, 1 hour, or until double in bulk. Brush tops with slightly beaten egg; sprinkle generously with sugar. Place in very hot oven (450°); lower heat to moderate (375°) at once. Bake 25 minutes, or until golden-brown. Cool slightly on wire racks. Slice each into 10 triangles.

Prune Filling

Combine ½ cup pitted dried prunes (from a 12-ounce package) and ½ cup water in a small saucepan. Simmer 30 minutes, or until prunes are very tender. Stir in ¼ cup sugar, then press mixture through a sieve or beat in an electric-blender container until smooth. Cool. Makes about ½ cup.

Almond Braid

A Kaffeeklatsch favorite with a sweet almond filling and crunchy almond topping.
Preheat oven to 450°, then lower heat to 375° and bake for 25 minutes. Makes 1 braid

Divide *Basic Danish Pastry* dough into quarters; chill or freeze three quarters to make into more braids or *Golden Pretzels* if you

wish. Roll out remaining quarter to a rectangle, 16x6, on a lightly floured pastry cloth or board; cut lengthwise into 3 two-inch-wide strips. Spread about 1 tablespoonful *Almond Filling* (recipe precedes) down middle of each; fold edges up over filling, pinching together to seal. Place the 3 filled strips on a greased cooky sheet; press together at one end; braid the three strips; press other ends together. Cover; let rise in a warm place, away from draft, 1 hour, or until double in bulk. Brush top with slightly beaten egg; sprinkle generously with sugar, then with about 1 tablespoon toasted shredded almonds (from a 5-ounce can). Place in very hot oven (450°); lower heat to moderate (375°) at once. Bake 25 minutes, or until golden-brown.

Golden Pretzel

The shape of this giant pretzel is often used as an insignia over a Danish bakeshop. Recipe makes two, each with a rich prune filling.
Preheat oven to 450°, then lower heat to 375° and bake for 20 minutes. Makes 2 large pretzels

Divide *Basic Danish Pastry* dough into quarters; chill or freeze three quarters to make into more pretzels or *Almond Braids*, if you wish. Divide remaining quarter in half. Roll out each to a long strip, 30x3, on a lightly floured pastry cloth or board. Spoon about ¼ cup *Prune Filling* (recipe precedes) down the middle of each, then fold one edge over filling to cover completely; overlap other edge over top ¼ inch. (Edges will open during baking.) Lift each filled strip carefully onto a greased cooky sheet; shape into a pretzel. Cover; let rise in a warm place, away from draft, 1 hour, or until double in bulk. Brush tops with slightly beaten egg; sprinkle generously with sugar, then with about ¼ cup toasted shredded almonds (from a 5-ounce can). Place in very hot oven (450°); lower heat to moderate (375°) at once. Bake 20 minutes, or until golden-brown.

Sunburst

Bake at 350° for 20 minutes. Makes 1 large coffee cake

1 package (13¾ ounces) hot-roll mix
10 tablespoons sugar
2 tablespoons vegetable shortening
2 eggs
¾ cup warm water

1 envelope (1 ounce) liquid unsweetened
  chocolate
1 teaspoon ground cinnamon
3 tablespoons butter or margarine, softened
½ cup chopped walnuts

1 Combine hot-roll mix, 2 tablespoons of the
sugar, and shortening in a large bowl; prepare
with 1 of the eggs and water, following label
directions. Cover with a clean towel. Let rise
in a warm place, away from draft, 1 hour, or
until double in bulk.
2 While dough rises, blend chocolate, remaining 8 tablespoons sugar, cinnamon, and butter
or margarine in a small bowl.
3 Punch dough down; turn out onto a lightly
floured pastry cloth or board. Knead 50 times,
or until smooth; cover again; let stand 10 minutes.
4 Roll out dough to a rectangle, 20x10; spread
chocolate mixture evenly over top; sprinkle ¼
cup of the walnuts over chocolate layer. Cut
rectangle in half lengthwise; starting at a long
side, roll up each half tightly, jelly-roll fashion.
5 Cut one roll into 6 equal pieces; cut 4 pieces,
the same size, from second roll. Twist remaining
piece into a coil and place in center of a lightly
greased large cooky sheet. Pinch ends of all
pieces to seal, then arrange around coil to form
a sunburst design.
6 Beat remaining egg slightly in a small bowl;
brush all over dough. Sprinkle remaining ¼ cup
walnuts over top; cover.
7 Let rise again in a warm place, away from
draft, 45 minutes, or until double in bulk.
8 Bake in moderate oven (350°) 20 minutes,
or until golden and loaf gives a hollow sound
when tapped. Remove from cooky sheet to a
wire rack. Serve warm or cold.

Herb Ring-A-Round
Ready-mixed salad herbs and nutmeg combine
for the tantalizing seasoner.
Bake at 375° for 20 minutes. Makes 1 nine-inch
round loaf

4 tablespoons (½ stick) butter or margarine
2 teaspoons mixed salad herbs
⅛ teaspoon nutmeg
2 packages (8 ounces each) refrigerated but-
  ter-flake or gem-flake rolls

1 Melt butter or margarine in a small saucepan;
stir in herbs and nutmeg.
2 Separate the dough in each package into 12
rolls; dip, 1 at a time, in butter mixture to coat
both sides. Stand on edge, working from outside toward center, in a single layer in a buttered
9-inch pie plate.

3 Bake in moderate oven (375°) 20 minutes,
or until golden. Break into serving-size pieces
with 2 forks. Serve hot.

Separate refrigerated rolls, give each a buttery
herb coat, and stand in their baker. To make
the prettiest loaf, work from outside to center

Ribbon Cheese Loaf
Zippy cheese bakes melty-golden between
layers of buttery rolls. Come summer, it's a
perfect partner for salads.
Bake at 375° for 45 minutes. Makes 1 loaf

2 packages (8 ounces each) refrigerated butterflake or gem-flake rolls
1 cup grated Cheddar cheese (4 ounces)
1 tablespoon melted butter or margarine
½ teaspoon dried parsley flakes

1 Separate the 12 rolls in each package, then
split each into 3 rounds. (It's easier if you work
with 8 rolls, or 24 rounds, enough for one layer
of the loaf, at a time. Rounds may not all be
evenly thick, but this will not affect the baking.)
2 Arrange the 24 rounds, overlapping slightly,
in 3 rows in bottom of a greased loaf pan, 9x5x3.
Sprinkle with half of the grated cheese. Top with
a second layer of 24 rounds, then remaining
cheese; cover with remaining 24 rounds.
3 Brush loaf with melted butter or margarine;
sprinkle evenly with parsley flakes.
4 Bake in moderate oven (375°) 45 minutes,
or until golden. Cut in slices; serve hot.

225

Petaled Honey Ring
Bake at 350° for 25 minutes. Makes 1 nine-inch
ring

2 packages (8 ounces each) refrigerated butterflake dinner rolls
3 tablespoons currants
3 teaspoons grated lemon rind

3 tablespoons honey
4 tablespoons (½ stick) butter or margarine, melted

1 Separate each package of rolls to make 24 even pieces. Place 12 pieces in a well-buttered 7-cup ring mold to make an even layer. Sprinkle 1 tablespoon of the currants and 1 teaspoon of the lemon rind over layer, then drizzle 1 tablespoon each of the honey and melted butter or margarine over top.
2 Make two more layers the same way; place remaining rolls on top. Drizzle remaining butter or margarine over all.
3 Bake in moderate oven (350°) 25 minutes, or until firm and golden. Loosen at once around edge with knife; invert onto a serving plate. Let stand 10 minutes. To serve, pull off layers with two forks; serve warm.

QUICK BREADS

Basic Muffins
Bake at 400° for 25 minutes. Makes 12 medium-size muffins

2 cups sifted all-purpose flour
2 tablespoons sugar
2 teaspoons baking powder
1 teaspoon salt
1 egg, beaten
1 cup milk
¼ cup melted butter or margarine

1 Sift flour, sugar, baking powder and salt into a medium-size bowl. Make a well in center of ingredients.
2 Combine egg, milk and melted butter or margarine in a small bowl; add all at once to flour mixture; stir lightly just until liquid is absorbed. (Batter will be lumpy.)
3 Spoon into 12 greased medium-size muffin-pan cups to fill ⅔ full.
4 Bake in a hot oven (400°) 25 minutes or until touched with brown and springy to the touch. Serve hot.

Whole Wheat Muffins
Bake at 400° for 25 minutes. Makes 12 medium-size muffins

1 cup sifted all-purpose flour
2 teaspoons baking powder

1 teaspoon salt
1 cup unsifted whole wheat flour
¼ cup molasses
1 egg, beaten
1 cup milk
¼ cup melted butter or margarine

1 Sift all-purpose flour, baking powder and salt into a medium-size bowl; stir in whole wheat flour and make a well in center of ingredients.
2 Combine molasses, egg, milk and melted butter or margarine in a small bowl; add all at once to flour mixture; stir lightly just until liquid is absorbed. (Batter will be lumpy.)
3 Spoon into 12 greased medium-sized muffin-pan cups to fill ⅔ full.
4 Bake in a hot oven (400°) 25 minutes or until golden brown and springy to the touch. Serve hot.

Bran Muffins
Bake at 400° for 20 minutes. Makes 12 medium-size muffins

2¼ cups whole bran
1 cup buttermilk
⅓ cup molasses
¼ cup firmly packed brown sugar
1 cup sifted all-purpose flour
1 teaspoon baking powder
1 teaspoon baking soda
1 teaspoon salt
1 egg, slightly beaten
¼ cup vegetable shortening, melted

1 Mix bran, buttermilk, molasses, and brown sugar in a small bowl; let stand until liquid is absorbed.
2 Sift flour, baking powder, soda, and salt into a large bowl.
3 Stir egg and melted shortening into bran mixture. Add all at once to flour mixture; stir lightly with a fork just until evenly moist. Spoon into greased medium-size muffin-pan cups, filling each ⅔ full.
4 Bake in hot oven (400°) 20 minutes, or until richly golden. Serve hot.

Corn Muffins
Bake at 400° for 20 minutes. Makes 12 medium-size muffins

1 cup sifted all-purpose flour
3 tablespoons sugar
1½ teaspoons baking powder
½ teaspoon baking soda
½ teaspoon salt
1 cup yellow or white corn meal

Two fruit-jeweled sweet breads, one (Petaled Honey Ring, background) to put together in a jiffy using commercial refrigerated dinner rolls, the other (Almond Foldovers, foreground) to make from scratch, knead, shape and bake.

Perfect Corn Muffins, golden brown and puffed, nutty and a little bit sweet. Serve them straight from the oven so that the butter will melt into them.

1 egg, well beaten
⅔ cup buttermilk
¼ cup vegetable shortening, melted

1 Sift flour, sugar, baking powder, soda, and salt into a large bowl; stir in corn meal.
2 Mix egg and buttermilk in a 1-cup measure; add all at once to flour mixture; stir lightly with a fork just until liquid is absorbed; stir in melted shortening.
3 Spoon into greased medium-size muffin-pan cups, filling each ⅔ full.
4 Bake in hot oven (400°) 20 minutes, or until golden. Serve hot.

228

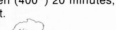

Wheat Germ Muffins

Doubly rich with old-fashioned molasses and nut-sweet wheat germ—and good for you, too
Bake at 400° for 30 minutes. Makes 12 medium-size muffins

1½ cups sifted all-purpose flour
¼ cup sugar
2 teaspoons baking powder
1 teaspoon salt
1 cup wheat germ (from a 12-ounce jar)
1 egg, well beaten
¾ cup milk
4 tablespoons (½ stick) butter or margarine, melted
¼ cup molasses

1 Sift flour, sugar, baking powder, and salt into medium-size bowl; stir in wheat germ.
2 Combine egg, milk, melted butter or margarine, and molasses in small bowl; add all at once to flour mixture; stir lightly just until liquid is absorbed. (Batter will be lumpy.)
3 Spoon into 12 greased medium-size muffin-pan cups to fill ⅔ full.
4 Bake in hot oven (400°) 30 minutes, or until richly browned; remove from pan at once; serve hot with butter or margarine and your favorite jelly, jam, marmalade, or preserves.

MUFFIN BAKERS: Try These Easy Tricks

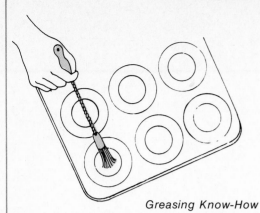

Greasing Know-How

Magic Oven

Melt shortening in each muffin cup (or use vegetable oil) and swish with a pastry brush. Or rub cups with the inside of a butter or margarine wrapper or a piece of buttered bread

Call on your electric skillet to freshen just a few muffins. The musts are a snug cover and low heat. Allow from 10 to 20 minutes, depending on size and quantity

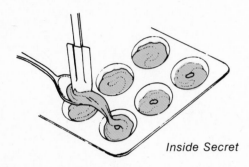

Inside Secret

Bottoms Up!

Next time you make plain muffins, hide a surprise in the center. Spoon part of batter into cups; add a dab of jelly or a cheese cube; top with remaining batter

If muffins are done ahead of serving time, loosen them from their cups, tilt slightly, then slide the pan back into the oven to stay warm. This keeps the muffins from steaming on the bottom.

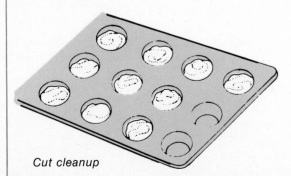

Cut cleanup

229

Made-to-Order Bakers

Not enough batter to fill your muffin pan? Pour some water into the empty cups or wipe out the grease so it doesn't scorch or turn the pan brown

Out of muffin pans? Bring out your metal jar rings—the kind used for canning—and place them on a cooky sheet. Set a paper baking cup in each; half-fill with batter and bake as usual. Or use your custard cups

BREADS

Baking Powder Biscuits

Bake at 425° for 12 minutes.
Makes 10 to 12 biscuits

2 cups sifted, all-purpose flour
3 teaspoons baking powder
1 teaspoon sugar
½ teaspoon salt
4 tablespoons vegetable shortening, butter, or margarine
¾ cup milk

1 Sift dry ingredients into a large bowl, then work in shortening until evenly mixed and crumbly. We use a metal mixing fork, but a pastry blender will do as well. Add milk all at once; stir lightly until dough is puffy-moist

2 Scoop dough out onto a lightly floured pastry cloth. Flour your hands a bit, pat dough into a thick square, then squeeze together. Knead 5 or 6 times so biscuits will rise evenly. Pat dough out to a square 1 inch thick.

3 Dip a 2-inch cutter into flour and cut out biscuits, working neatly from rim to middle so there will be few scraps to reroll. Set the rounds 1 inch apart on greased cooky sheet and bake in hot oven (425°) 12 minutes, or until golden.

Baking Powder Biscuits

1 Combine biscuit mix and sage in a medium-size bowl; cut in butter or margarine until mixture is crumbly. Add milk and grated onion; prepare, following label directions for rolled biscuits.

2 Divide into 18 pieces; roll each into a rope, 12 inches long. Braid each 3 ropes, pinching at ends to hold in place.

3 Place 3 braids, side by side, on a cooky sheet, shaping ends to an oval. Top with 2 more ropes for middle layer; place remaining on top. Brush all over with beaten egg.

4 Bake in moderate oven (375°) 1 hour, or until golden. Serve warm.

●

Cheddar Biscuits

Tucked into each quick-mix biscuit is a cube of sharp cheese. Recipe gives a slick shaping hint.
Bake at 450° for 12 minutes. Makes 12 biscuits

2 cups biscuit mix
Milk
12 cubes sharp Cheddar cheese (from a 6-ounce package)

1 Prepare biscuit mix with milk, following label directions for 12 biscuits. Turn out onto lightly floured pastry cloth or board; knead 8 to 10 times.

2 Roll dough out to a rectangle, 12x8; place 12 cubes of cheese, about 1½ inches apart in

●

Sage Dinner Braid

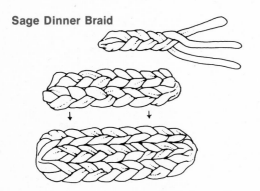

Start with 18 "ropes" of dough; braid by threes. Then stack them, pyramid style, with three braids on bottom, two in middle, and a single one on top.

Sage Dinner Braid

Biscuit dough is rolled into ropes, then stacked to make this inviting loaf.
Bake at 375° for 1 hour. Makes 1 large loaf

4 cups biscuit mix
1 teaspoon ground sage
½ cup (1 stick) butter or margarine
1⅓ cups milk
2 teaspoons grated onion
1 egg, slightly beaten

3 rows of 4 each, on half of dough; fold other half over to make a second layer:

3 Cut into 12 about-2-inch squares, cutting between cubes of cheese; place on greased cooky sheet.

4 Bake in very hot oven (450°) 12 minutes, or until richly golden.

Onion Kuchen

Creamy-rich onion topper bakes over biscuits for this late-breakfast or supper hot bread.
Bake at 375° for 30 minutes. Makes 8 servings

2 medium-size onions, peeled, sliced, and separated into rings
3 tablespoons butter or margarine
1 package (8 ounces) refrigerated home-style or buttermilk biscuits
1 egg
1 cup (8-ounce carton) dairy sour cream
½ teaspoon salt
1 teaspoon poppy seeds

1 Sauté onions slowly in butter or margarine just until soft in a medium-size frying pan.

2 Separate the 10 biscuits; place in a single layer in an ungreased 8-inch layer-cake pan, pressing together to cover bottom completely. (Or, if you want to remove loaf from pan for party serving, bake in an 8-inch spring-form pan.) Spoon onion mixture on top.

3 Beat egg slightly in a small bowl; blend in sour cream and salt. Spoon over onion mixture; sprinkle with poppy seeds.

4 Bake in moderate oven (375°) 30 minutes, or until topping is set. Slice in wedges; serve warm.

Miniature Dill Loaves

Served piping-hot, this herb-seasoned bread dresses any meal in grand style.
Bake at 375° for 30 minutes. Makes 3 little loaves

Onion Kuchen looks like a complicated recipe but it isn't because it is built zip-quick out of commercial refrigerated biscuits.

1 package (8 ounces) refrigerated flaky biscuits
4 tablespoons (½ stick) butter or margarine, melted
½ teaspoon dill weed

1 Separate the 12 biscuits; dip each into melted butter or margarine in a pie plate. Stand 4 each into ungreased toy-size loaf pans; sprinkle with dill weed. Place pans on a cooky sheet for easy handling, if you wish.

2 Bake in moderate oven (375°) 30 minutes, or until golden. Serve hot.

NOTE—If you do not have toy-size loaf pans, make your own by shaping a double thickness of foil to 4x2½x1½ size.

Miniature Lemon-Sugar Loaves

One package makes three loaves. Each person breaks off his own roll-size serving.
Bake at 375° for 30 minutes. Makes 3 little loaves

½ cup sugar
5 teaspoons grated lemon rind
4 tablespoons (½ stick) butter or margarine, melted

1 package (8 ounces) refrigerated flaky biscuits

1 Mix sugar and lemon rind on wax paper or foil; place melted butter or margarine in a pie plate.
2 Separate the 12 biscuits; dip each into melted butter or margarine, then in sugar mixture to coat well. Stand 4 each into ungreased toy-size loaf pans. Place pans on a cooky sheet for easy handling, if you wish.
3 Bake in moderate oven (375°) 30 minutes, or until golden. Serve hot.
Note—If you do not have toy-size loaf pans, make your own by shaping a double thickness of foil to 4x2½x1½ size.

Popovers
Bake at 400° F. for 50 minutes. Makes 8 large popovers.

2 eggs
1 cup milk
1 cup sifted all-purpose flour
½ teaspoon salt

1 Heat oven to 400° F. Heavily butter 8 six-ounce custard cups; place on baking sheet for easy handling; slide into hot oven to heat while mixing batter.
2 Beat eggs slightly in bowl or 1-quart measure; add remaining ingredients; beat briskly ½ minute; scrape beater and sides of bowl; beat ½ minute longer. Batter will be creamy-smooth and rather thin.
3 Pour into heated custard cups, filling each ⅓ full to allow room for popping.
4 Bake in hot oven (400° F.) 50 minutes, or until popped, crisp, and golden-brown. *Do not peek during baking, for they may fall.* Serve hot with butter or margarine and jam.

232

Old-Fashioned Corn Bread
Bake at 425° for 20 minutes. Makes 12 sticks, 12 muffins, or 1 nine-inch square loaf

1½ cups yellow or white corn meal
1½ teaspoons baking powder
1 teaspoon salt
¾ teaspoon baking soda
1 egg
1½ cups buttermilk
¼ cup vegetable shortening, melted

1 Measure dry ingredients into large bowl; mix with a fork. (No need to sift corn meal.) Beat egg into buttermilk; stir in to make a thin smooth batter
2 Pour melted shortening into cornmeal mixture; stir to blend. To make crust crisp, heat greased corn-stick, muffin, or 9x9x2 pan while mixing up batter
3 Pour batter in hot pan. Bake in hot oven (425°) 20 minutes for sticks and muffins, 25 minutes for square loaf, or until crusty and golden-brown. Serve hot

Irish Soda Bread
Sugary syrup lightly "frosts" this fruity bread during last few minutes of baking.
Bake at 375° for 55 minutes. Makes 1 round loaf

3 cups sifted all-purpose flour
3 tablespoons sugar (for dough)
3 teaspoons baking powder
½ teaspoon baking soda
½ teaspoon salt
1 cup dried currants
1⅓ cups buttermilk
2 tablespoons sugar (for glaze)
2 tablespoons hot water

1 Sift flour, 3 tablespoons sugar, baking powder, soda, and salt into medium-size bowl; stir in currants, then buttermilk until blended. (Dough will be sticky.)
2 Turn out onto lightly floured pastry cloth or board; knead about 10 times. Shape into an 8-inch round loaf; place on ungreased cooky sheet. Cut a cross in top of dough with sharp knife.
3 Bake in moderate oven (375°) 45 minutes; remove from oven.
4 Dissolve 2 tablespoons sugar in hot water in a cup; brush generously over hot loaf. Bake 10 minutes longer, or until richly golden. Serve warm.

Sage Sticks
Bake at 425° for 10 minutes. Makes 4 dozen

1 cup sifted all-purpose flour
1½ teaspoons baking powder
½ teaspoon salt
½ teaspoon leaf sage, crumbled
½ cup grated mild Cheddar cheese
2 tablespoons butter or margarine
⅓ cup cold water

1 Sift flour, baking powder, and salt into a medium-size bowl; stir in sage and cheese; cut in butter or margarine with a pastry blender until mixture is crumbly. Sprinkle water over top; mix lightly with a fork just until pastry holds together and leaves side of bowl clean.

2 Roll out to a rectangle, 12x10, on a lightly floured pastry cloth or board. Divide in half lengthwise, then cut each half crosswise into ½-inch-wide strips. Place, 1 inch apart, on un-greased cooky sheets.

3 Bake in hot oven (425°) 10 minutes, or until lightly golden. Remove from cooky sheets; cool on wire racks. Store in a tightly covered container.

Golden Cheese Bread

Whole-wheat cereal blends with cheese in this mellow quick bread. If you have any left over, toast for breakfast.
Bake at 400° for 30 minutes. Makes 1 loaf

1¼ cups sifted all-purpose flour
2 tablespoons sugar
3 teaspoons baking powder
½ teaspoon salt
¾ cup uncooked granulated instant whole-wheat cereal
1 cup grated Cheddar cheese (4 ounces)
1 egg
¾ cup milk
¼ cup vegetable oil

1 Sift flour, sugar, baking powder, and salt into a medium-size bowl; stir in cereal and cheese.
2 Beat egg with milk and vegetable oil in a small bowl; add all at once to flour mixture, stirring just until blended. Pour into a greased loaf pan, 9x5x3.
3 Bake in hot oven (400°) 30 minutes, or until golden and a wooden pick inserted in middle comes out clean. Cool 5 minutes on a wire rack, then turn out. Slice and serve while still warm.

Apple-Walnut Bread

Bake at 350° for 1 hour and 10 minutes. Makes 1 loaf, 9x5x3

3 cups sifted all-purpose flour
¾ cup sugar
3 teaspoons baking powder
1 teaspoon salt
½ teaspoon cinnamon
2 cups diced pared apple
½ cup finely chopped walnuts
1 egg
¾ cup milk
3 tablespoons vegetable shortening, melted

1 Sift flour, sugar, baking powder, salt, and cinnamon into a large bowl; stir in diced apple and walnuts to mix well. Beat the egg slightly with milk and shortening in a small bowl
2 Pour all at once into flour mixture; stir just until evenly moist. (Work with a light hand, for heavy—or too much—stirring will cause the baked bread to have small tunnels in it)
3 Spoon batter into a well-greased loaf pan, 9x5x3, then spread to sides of pan with a spoon, leaving a slight well in center. This helps loaf rise evenly with no hump in middle
4 Bake in moderate oven (350°) 1 hour and 10 minutes, or until wooden pick inserted in center comes out clean and loaf pulls away from sides of pan. Remove from pan; cool

Date Tea Bread

It's dark, moist, and mellow-rich.
Bake at 350° for 1 hour and 10 minutes. Makes 1 loaf, 9x5x3

1 package (8 ounces) pitted dates
1¼ cups boiling water
1½ cups firmly packed brown sugar
6 tablespoons (¾ stick) butter or margarine
1 egg, beaten
2¼ cups sifted all-purpose flour
1½ teaspoons baking soda
1½ teaspoons salt

1 Cut dates in small pieces into medium-size bowl; pour boiling water over. Stir in sugar and butter or margarine until butter melts; cool. Stir in beaten egg.
2 Sift flour, soda, and salt onto wax paper; stir into date mixture just until blended. Pour into greased loaf pan, 9x5x3; let stand 15 minutes.
3 Bake in moderate oven (350°) 1 hour and 10 minutes, or until wooden pick inserted deep into loaf comes out clean. Cool in pan 5 minutes; turn out on wire rack; cool completely.
4 Wrap in wax paper, foil, or transparent wrap; store at least 1 day before slicing.

Polka-Dot Raisin Log

Bake at 350° for 30 minutes. Makes 1 loaf, 9x5x3

1½ cups biscuit mix
¼ cup firmly packed light brown sugar
1 teaspoon grated orange rind
2 eggs
¼ cup water
½ cup semisweet-chocolate pieces

233

BREADS

¼ cup chopped pecans
¼ cup seedless raisins
½ cup 10X (confectioners' powdered)
   sugar
   Few drops vanilla

1 Combine biscuit mix, brown sugar, and orange rind in a large bowl. Vigorously stir in eggs and water; fold in chocolate pieces, pecans, and raisins.
2 Spoon into a generously buttered 5-cup mold or loaf pan, 9x5x3; spread top even. (If you're using a loaf pan, baked loaf will fill pan only halfway.)
3 Bake in moderate oven (350°) 30 minutes, or until puffed and golden. Loosen around edge with a knife; invert onto a wire rack.
4 Combine 10X sugar, vanilla, and 2 teaspoons water in a cup; blend until smooth and easy to pour from a spoon. Drizzle over loaf, letting mixture drip down side. Let stand until glaze sets. Slice crosswise; serve warm or cold.

Cranberry-Pecan Bread
Bake at 350° for 1 hour and 10 minutes. Makes 1 nine-inch round loaf

1½ cups chopped pecans

1½ cups coarsely ground cranberries
1¼ cups sugar
 3 cups sifted all-purpose flour
4½ teaspoons baking powder
 ½ teaspoon salt
 ½ cup vegetable shortening
 2 teaspoons grated lemon rind
 2 eggs
 1 cup milk

1 Grease a 9-inch angle-cake pan; sprinkle ½ cup of the pecans evenly over bottom.
2 Mix cranberries and ¼ cup of the sugar in a small bowl; let stand while preparing batter.
3 Sift flour, remaining 1 cup sugar, baking powder, and salt into a large bowl; cut in shortening with a pastry blender until mixture resembles corn meal. Stir in remaining 1 cup pecans and lemon rind.
4 Beat eggs well in a small bowl; stir in milk. Add all at once to flour mixture; stir just until evenly moist. Spoon into prepared pan; spread top even.
5 Bake in moderate oven (350°) 1 hour and 10 minutes, or until a wooden pick inserted near center comes out clean. Cool in pan on a wire rack 10 minutes. Loosen around edge and center with a knife; turn out onto rack. Cool loaf completely.
6 Wrap loaf in wax paper, foil, or transparent

A particularly popular fruit-nut bread, and certainly one of the most colorful: Cranberry-Pecan Bread.

wrap. Store overnight to mellow flavors and make slicing easier. Cut in thin wedges.

Cinnamon-Prune Bread
Bake at 350° for 1 hour and 5 minutes. Makes 1 loaf, 9x5x3

    1 cup pitted prunes, chopped (from a 12-ounce package)
    ½ cup boiling water
    3 cups sifted all-purpose flour
    4½ teaspoons baking powder
    ½ teaspoon salt
    ½ teaspoon ground cinnamon
    ⅔ cup firmly packed brown sugar
    1 tablespoon grated orange rind
    1 cup chopped pecans
    1 egg
    ¼ cup vegetable oil
    ¾ cup milk

1 Grease a loaf pan, 9x5x3.
2 Combine prunes and boiling water in a small bowl; let stand while preparing batter.
3 Sift flour, baking powder, salt, and cinnamon into a large bowl; stir in brown sugar, orange rind, and pecans.
4 Beat egg well in a medium-size bowl; stir in vegetable oil, milk, and prune mixture. Add all at once to flour mixture; stir just until evenly moist. Spoon into prepared pan; spread top even.
5 Bake in moderate oven (350°) 1 hour and 5 minutes, or until a wooden pick inserted in center comes out clean. Cool in pan on a wire rack 10 minutes. Loosen around edges with a knife; turn out onto rack. Cool completely.
6 Wrap loaf in wax paper, foil, or transparent wrap. Store overnight to mellow flavors and make slicing easier. Cut in thin slices.

Honey-Spice Ring
Light as spongecake, this loaf is flecked with candied orange peel.
Bake at 350° for 45 minutes. Makes 1 nine-inch ring

    2 cups sifted all-purpose flour
    1 teaspoon ground cloves
    1 teaspoon ground ginger
    ½ teaspoon baking powder
    4 eggs
    1 cup firmly packed brown sugar
    ⅓ cup honey
    ¼ cup coarsely chopped candied orange peel

1 Sift flour, spices, and baking powder onto wax paper.

2 Beat eggs until foamy in a large bowl; sprinkle in brown sugar, beating until fluffy; beat in honey. (Beating will take about 15 minutes altogether with an electric beater.)
3 Fold in orange peel, then flour mixture just until blended. Spoon into an ungreased 9-inch tube pan.
4 Bake in moderate oven (350°) 45 minutes, or until top springs back when pressed with fingertip. Invert pan, hanging tube over a bottle; cool bread completely.
5 Remove from pan to a serving plate. Cut in thin wedges.

PANCAKES AND WAFFLES

Pancakes
Makes 6 servings

    2 cups sifted all-purpose flour
    3 teaspoons baking powder
    1 tablespoon sugar
    2 eggs, well beaten
    1½ cups milk
    2 tablespoons vegetable oil or melted vegetable shortening

1 Sift flour, baking powder and sugar onto a piece of wax paper.
2 Combine eggs and milk in a medium-size mixing bowl.
3 Add sifted dry ingredients to the egg-milk mixture and beat until smooth; stir in vegetable oil or melted shortening.
4 Bake on a medium hot griddle and serve immediately.

Step-by-Step to Perfect Pancakes

1 Make sure griddle is just-right hot before adding the batter. Here's how to test it: Sprinkle on several drops of water; when they sputter and dance about, grease griddle and start pouring

2 For even-size pancakes, measure batter, using a scant quarter cup for a 4-inch round. The batter spreads, so leave a little space between cakes and they will keep their shape and be easy to turn

3 When pancakes look puffy and slightly dry around edge, bubbles cover the top, and the underside is golden, flip them over with a wide spatula. Bake a few minutes more, or until bottoms brown

235

BREADS

4 If pancakes must stand before serving, keep them hot this undercover way. Place in a pie plate, turn a colander upside-down over top, and set in a warm place. Heat stays in, steam wafts out.

Buttermilk Griddle Cakes
Makes 6 servings

2 cups sifted all-purpose flour
1 teaspoon baking soda
1 teaspoon salt
1 tablespoon sugar
2 eggs, well beaten
2 cups buttermilk
2 tablespoons vegetable oil or melted vegetable shortening

1 Sift flour, baking soda, salt and sugar onto a piece of wax paper.
2 Combine eggs and buttermilk in a medium-size mixing bowl.
3 Add sifted dry ingredients to the buttermilk mixture and beat until smooth; stir in vegetable oil or melted shortening.
4 Bake on a medium hot griddle and serve immediately.

Waffles
Makes 6 waffles

2 cups sifted all-purpose flour
2 teaspoons baking powder
½ teaspoon salt
3 tablespoons sugar
2 eggs, separated
1¼ cups milk
6 tablespoons vegetable oil or melted vegetable shortening

1 Sift flour with baking powder, salt and sugar onto a large piece of wax paper.
2 Beat egg whites until stiff but not dry; set aside.
3 Beat egg yolks well in a medium-size bowl and stir in milk.
4 Add sifted dry ingredients and mix just enough to blend; add vegetable oil or melted shortening. Fold in egg whites.
5 Bake in a moderately hot waffle iron 4 to 5 minutes until crisp and brown or as iron manufacturer directs. Serve hot with melted butter and syrup or honey.

The all-American favorite: a huge stack of pancakes, topped with a melting pat of butter and old-fashioned maple syrup.

FRITTERS AND FRIED BREADS

Yeast-Raised Doughnuts
Makes about 2 dozen

3¾ to 4¾ cups unsifted all-purpose flour
½ cup sugar
1 teaspoon salt
¼ teaspoon ground cinnamon
⅛ teaspoon ground mace
2 envelopes active dry yeast
1 cup very warm potato cooking water
¼ cup (½ stick) butter or margarine, melted
½ cup lukewarm mashed potatoes
1 egg
   Vegetable oil or vegetable shortening for deep fat frying
   10X (confectioners' powdered) sugar

1 Mix 1½ cups flour, the sugar, salt, spices, undissolved active dry yeast in a large mixing bowl.
2 Combine very warm potato cooking water and melted butter or margarine. (Very warm potato cooking water should feel comfortably warm when dropped on wrist.) Add gradually to flour mixture and beat 2 minutes at medium speed of electric mixer, scraping sides of bowl often.
3 Add potatoes, egg and ½ cup flour—or enough to make a stiff batter. Beat at high speed 2 minutes, scraping bowl occasionally. Stir in enough additional flour to make a soft dough.
4 Turn onto a lightly floured board and knead until smooth and elastic, about 10 minutes, adding only enough flour to keep dough from sticking.
5 Place in a greased bowl, turn to grease all over, cover with a clean towel and let rise in a warm place, away from draft, until double in bulk, about 1 hour.
6 Punch dough down, turn onto a lightly floured board and roll to a thickness of ½ inch. Cut with a lightly floured 3-inch doughnut cutter.
7 Place doughnuts on lightly greased baking sheets, cover with clean towels and let rise again in a warm spot, away from draft, until double in bulk, about ½ hour.
8 Fry in deep hot fat (375°) until golden brown on both sides. Drain on paper toweling and dust with 10X sugar.

Quick Spicy Doughnuts
Makes about 2 dozen

3 cups pancake mix
⅔ cup sugar
1 teaspoon ground cinnamon
¼ teaspoon ground ginger
¼ teaspoon ground allspice
¼ teaspoon ground nutmeg
2 eggs, well beaten
¾ cup milk
2 tablespoons melted butter or margarine
   Vegetable oil or vegetable shortening for deep fat frying
   Cinnamon-sugar

1 Mix pancake mix, sugar and spices together in a medium-size mixing bowl.
2 Combine eggs and milk, add to dry ingredients and mix well; stir in melted butter or margarine.
3 Roll dough on a lightly floured board to a thickness of ½" and cut with a lightly floured 3-inch doughnut cutter.
4 Fry in deep hot fat (375°) until golden brown on both sides. Drain on paper toweling and sprinkle with cinnamon-sugar.

Corn Fritters
Makes about 1 dozen

1 cup sifted all-purpose flour
1 teaspoon baking powder
1 teaspoon sugar
½ teaspoon salt
2 eggs, well beaten
½ cup milk
1 teaspoon vegetable oil
1 cup cooked or canned whole kernel corn, well drained
   Vegetable oil or vegetable shortening for deep fat frying

1 Sift flour, baking powder, sugar and salt onto a piece of wax paper.
2 Combine eggs and milk in a medium-size mixing bowl; add sifted dry ingredients and beat lightly to mix; stir in 1 teaspoon vegetable oil and the corn.
3 Drop from a tablespoon into deep hot fat (375°) and fry until golden brown on all sides. Drain on paper toweling and serve at once.

237

COMMERCIAL BREADS: SOME BASICS AND BUYING TIPS

BREAD IS EVERYWHERE

Look around your supermarket. There's hardly a spot that doesn't stock some kind of bread. The baked-goods department is invitingly large with breads, rolls, and muffins of many shapes, sizes, varieties, and brands. In the grocery section are canned brown bread, nut loaves, and specialty fruit breads. Refrigerated cabinets hold quick-to-bake biscuits and rolls in a tube. And among the frozen foods you'll find everything from ready-to-bake roll and bread doughs to ready-to-eat baked fancies.

THE LABEL TELLS THE STORY

Never be fooled by a big bouncy loaf or a lot of slices, for bread is sold by weight, clearly marked on the label. Read it so you'll know what you are paying for. Frequently your supermarket's newspaper ads list bread specials with the weights and prices, and it's a good practice to check them so you'll know the best buys by size and brand names.

THE OLD SQUEEZE PLAY IS OUT

Varieties of breads differ in softness and firmness, even when freshly baked. There's seldom need to squeeze the loaf to see if it is soft, for many bakers proudly indicate freshness by dating each loaf on an end seal.

IS ALL BREAD ENRICHED?

No, but most white bread is. In simple terms, "enrichment" means that valuable protein, minerals, and B vitamins taken out of wheat when it's milled into white flour are put back in. About 30 states require enrichment, but most bakers in other states voluntarily buy flour that is enriched so their breads, without adding extra cost or calories, are just as nutritionally rich.

238

WHAT WOULD WE DO WITHOUT BREAD?

Bread is as much a mainstay around the clock as it is for luncheon sandwiches and breakfast toast. Here are about a dozen ways of using it in all kinds of dishes, from dinner starters through desserts.

• **Appetizer Bases**—Cut bread into little squares and toast in a moderate oven (350°) 15 minutes, or until golden. Use with cheese and meat spreads or as scoops for dips.

• **Casseroles**—For toppings, cut sliced bread into tiny cubes or pull apart into crumbs, toss with melted butter or margarine, grated cheese, or mixed dry herbs, then sprinkle over the top of your casserole before baking. Or slice French bread very thin, butter slices, and place, overlapping, around the rim of the casserole. French bread, too, can be the base for a main dish.

• **Meat**—Many meat-loaf and meat-ball recipes call for soft bread crumbs, and, of course, white bread is the stand-by. But for variety, try rye with caraway seeds, white with a sesame-seed topping, or whole-wheat or cheese breads.

• **Soup, Salad, Vegetable Toppers**—Croutons sprinkled on top of soup or a green salad bowl or creamed vegetables add a company touch—and it's easy to have them on hand. Just cut bread into about-½-inch cubes and toast the same as for appetizer bases. Store in a tightly covered container.

• **Desserts**—Bread pudding and fruit Bettys, favorites of generations ago, are just as popular today, and French or raisin breads taste equally delicious as white bread. If yours is a French-toast-loving family, try it as dessert topped with a generous sprinkle of cinnamon-sugar or confectioners' sugar and sliced strawberries or peaches.

Q AND A ON BREAD

Q. Which is better—white or whole-wheat bread?

A. Both have about the same whole-grain goodness since most white breads are enriched, but whole-wheat has more bulk and a more nutlike flavor. For mealtime variety, use both.

Q. Is there a special bread for weight-watchers?

A. Some breads come in smaller loaves with thinner slices, so naturally the calorie count per slice will be lower than for a thick slice from a large loaf. If you are on a calorie-trimming diet, don't slight bread, because it gives you needed protein, some B vitamins, and iron. And remember, no one food will make you fat or thin. It's how much you eat that counts.

Q. Do supermarkets really mark down the price of day-old bread?

A. Most do on their own private brands, and as both fresh and day-old prices are marked on the products, it's easy to spot the bargains. Big bakeries that deliver to supermarkets usually take back any unsold bread to offer at a lower price in their own thrift departments.

Q. Should frozen bread be thawed before making into sandwiches for lunch boxes?

A. It's actually easier to work with frozen bread, for slices can be spread more easily without tearing. Tightly wrapped, the sandwiches will help to keep other foods in the lunch box cold, and by lunchtime the bread will be thawed and invitingly fresh-tasting.

Q. I read a lot about sour-dough bread. What is it?

A. This bread is made of flour, water, and salt, but no yeast or shortening. Its leavening is a special starter called a "sour ferment." The loaf has a light brown blistery crust, a firm crumb similar to French bread, and a pleasantly tangy flavor. For best eating, serve it hot.

SOME TIPS ON STORING BREAD

In a Bread Box: Always leave breads in their original wrappers or if they're home-made, wrap in transparent wrap. Keep bread box spotlessly clean and place it in a clean, cool, dry, well ventilated area. Avoid, particularly, storing near dishwashers or laundry appliances which increase both the temperature and the humidity, courting mold growth. In hot and humid weather, increase ventilation in bread box by leaving cover ajar, if necessary.

In the Refrigerator: Best not. Refrigeration actually *speeds* staling. Use refrigerator only as a last resort in hot, muggy weather to keep bread from molding.

In the Freezer: An ideal way to keep breads, particularly home-made breads which can be baked in cool weather and put away for summer. Wrap well in transparent wrap, label (including date) and store at 0° or lower. *To use frozen bread:* Unwrap and thaw at room temperature, then heat, uncovered, in a hot oven (400°) for about five minutes. Serve immediately.

SOME WAYS TO JAZZ UP STORE-BOUGHT BREADS

Little Garlic Loaves
Each serving looks like a ready-sliced miniature loaf.
Bake at 350° for 10 minutes. Makes 6 servings

1 loaf long thin French bread
6 tablespoons (¾ stick) butter or margarine
1 clove of garlic, peeled and quartered

1 Cut bread into ¼-inch-thick slices almost through to bottom crust, then divide into 6 equal-size "loaves."
2 Melt butter or margarine with garlic in a small saucepan; remove garlic. Brush butter or margarine generously onto cut surfaces of each slice; re-form into a long loaf; wrap loosely in foil.

3 Bake in moderate oven (350°) 10 minutes, or until heated through. Unwrap and pile into a napkin-lined basket to keep warm.

CRISPY HOT BREADS

Club Toasties
Make 4 to 5 deep cuts diagonally in brown'n'serve club rolls; spread cuts generously with butter or margarine mixed with chopped parsley. Bake, following label directions. Or start with ready-baked rolls, spread, and simply toast in oven

Olive-Cheese Rounds
Roll refrigerated biscuits (plain or buttermilk) to 3-inch rounds. Drizzle with melted butter or margarine, then top each with several thin slices of Cheddar cheese and sliced ripe olives. Place on a greased cooky sheet. Bake in hot oven (400°) 10 minutes, or until cheese melts and bubbles

239

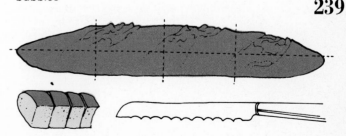

Garlic-Bread Chunks
Halve a loaf of French bread lengthwise, then quarter crosswise. Make 3 cuts in each piece

almost to bottom crust; spread with butter or margarine seasoned with minced garlic or garlic powder. Place on a cooky sheet. Bake in hot oven (425°) 5 minutes, or until crispy-hot

Cracker Crunchies
Split milk crackers with a small sharp-tip knife. Brush with melted butter or margarine; sprinkle with seasoned salt. Place on a cooky sheet. Bake in hot oven (400°) 10 minutes, or until toasty-crisp. Other topping ideas: Diced cooked bacon, mixed salad herbs, Italian seasoning

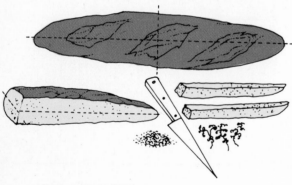

Italian Herb Sticks
Halve a loaf of Italian bread lengthwise and crosswise, then split each quarter. Brush cut sides with melted butter or margarine mixed with oregano or basil. Place on a cooky sheet. Bake in hot oven (425°) 5 minutes, or until toasty. (Grated Parmesan cheese is delicious, too)

Fan-Tan Loaves
Separate refrigerated butterflake or gem flake rolls into 12 pieces; stand 4 each in ungreased toy loaf pans. Brush with melted butter or margarine; sprinkle with celery or sesame seeds. Bake in moderate oven (375°) 30 minutes, or until golden

240

SWEET SNACKS WITH STORE-BOUGHT BREAD

Each of these hot crispy bites starts with sliced or French bread or English muffins. All are quick to fix, ready to eat in minutes, and so good with coffee, tea, or milk

Peanut Toasties—Blend 4 tablespoons (½ stick) butter or margarine and ¼ cup creamy peanut butter in a bowl; stir in ¼ cup chopped walnuts and 3 tablespoons honey. Spread on 6 slices toasted whole-wheat bread; place on cooky sheet. Broil 3 to 4 minutes, or until topping bubbles and browns lightly. Cut in quarters. Makes 4 servings

Ginger-Orange Rounds—Blend 6 tablespoons (¾ stick) butter or margarine with ⅓ cup orange marmalade in a small bowl; stir in ¼ cup toasted slivered almonds and ⅛ teaspoon ground ginger. Spread on 4 toasted split English muffins; place on a cooky sheet. Broil 3 to 4 minutes, or until topping bubbles up. Makes 4 servings

Apricot Foldovers—Mix 1 package (3 or 4 ounces) cream cheese and ¼ cup apricot jam in a bowl. Spread 1 tablespoon on each of 10 slices white bread; fold diagonally; press edges to seal. Place on cooky sheet; brush with cream; sprinkle with sugar and coconut. Bake in hot oven (400°) 10 minutes, or until toasted. Makes 4 to 6 servings

Maple-Honey Toast—Cut 8 half-inch-thick slices from a loaf of French bread. Melt 4 tablespoons (½ stick) butter or margarine in a large frying pan; stir in ¼ cup maple-honey-flavor syrup; heat until bubbly. Place bread slices in a single layer in pan; saute, turning often, until golden and richly glazed. Serve hot. Makes 4 servings

Cinnamon Rollups—Blend 4 tablespoons (½ stick) butter or margarine, ½ cup brown sugar, and 1 teaspoon cinnamon in a bowl. Trim crusts from 8 slices white bread; roll out flat; spread with butter mixture; roll up; place on a cooky sheet. Brush with melted butter. Bake in hot oven (425°) 10 minutes, or until toasted. Makes 8 servings

Apple-Raisin Pudding—Trim crusts from 7 slices toasted raisin bread; cut 1 slice into thirds. Line pan, 8x4x2, with 2 slices and 1 strip; top with ⅔ cup apple-pie filling (it'll take a 1-pound, 5-ounce can); repeat layers twice. Bake in moderate oven (375°) 40 minutes, or until hot. Turn out; serve with cream. Makes 4 servings

HOW TO MAKE BREAD CRUMBS

Soft Bread Crumbs: Tear slices of bread into small pieces with your fingers.

Dry Bread Crumbs: Put dry bread slices through a food chopper fitted with a fine blade. A neat trick is to tie a paper bag on the blade end of the grinder so that the crumbs will drop directly into the bag as they are ground—no mess. *For Fine Crumbs:* Sift the ground crumbs through a fine sieve. Store the fine crumbs and the coarse (those left behind in the sieve) separately in covered containers.

Buttered Bread Crumbs: Melt ⅓ cup butter or margarine in a skillet, add 1 cup dry bread crumbs and stir—fry until crumbs are golden brown. Makes 1 cup buttered crumbs.

HOW TO MAKE BREAD CUBES AND CROUTONS

Soft Bread Cubes: Stack two or three slices of bread on a cutting board and cut into strips of desired width, then cut across the strips to form cubes of even size.

Toasted Bread Cubes: Spread soft bread cubes out on a baking sheet and set in a slow oven (300°). Toast, turning occasionally, until golden brown on all sides.

Croutons: Brown soft bread cubes, about ½ cup at a time, in about ½ inch of melted butter or margarine or olive oil in a large heavy skillet over moderately high heat, stirring and turning often, until evenly golden brown on all sides. *For Garlic Croutons:* Warm 1 crushed clove garlic in the melted butter or margarine or olive oil until golden; remove before frying croutons.

SOME BREAD MEASUREMENTS

1 (⅝-inch) slice fresh bread = 1 cup soft bread cubes

1 (⅝-inch) slice dry bread = ¾ cup dry bread cubes

1 (⅝-inch) slice fresh bread = ¾ cup toasted bread cubes

1 (⅝-inch) slice fresh bread = 1 cup soft bread crumbs

1 (⅝-inch) slice dry bread = ⅓ cup dry bread crumbs

241

What a beautiful way to start the day: stacks of pancakes, sausage links and melons mounded with berries.

BREAKFAST—GETTING A GOOD HEADSTART ON THE DAY:
THE IMPORTANCE OF BREAKFAST, SHOPPING AND STORING TIPS FOR BREAKFAST CEREALS, MENUS, RECIPES

THE IMPORTANCE OF BREAKFAST

The best way to start the day right is by eating a good breakfast. A great many people don't because the idea of food first thing in the morning turns them off, even though "good breakfast" isn't synonymous with "heavy breakfast."

What *is* a good breakfast? One that:

—Supplies about one-fourth of the day's total food intake.

—Provides protein (meat, fish, cheese, eggs, milk), minerals and vitamins, particularly vitamin C (citrus fruits, berries, melons, tomatoes) and the B group (cereals and grains).

—Furnishes the body with energy (calories).

—Looks and tastes good.

Black coffee on-the-run doesn't qualify. Nor do coffee and doughnuts or Danish. Danes, by the way, go in for hearty breakfasts—cheeses, cold cuts, fruits, eggs, assorted breads (both sweet and savory), milk, coffee. *Very* good breakfasts.

In America, breakfast, more than any other meal, tends to be ho-hum. Few people are imaginative about breakfast and fall into the same-thing-every-morning rut. No need to. There's nothing wrong, for example, with serving steak for breakfast (in the hell-for-leather cowboy days, it was standard breakfast fare). Down South, people like thick pink slices of country ham with grits and "red-eye" (ham) gravy. In the Midwest, breakfasts run to sausages and home-fried potatoes or apples. Not bad as breakfasts go, though heavier than many people would want—or need.

Those most apt to miss out on breakfast are dieters. *But* breakfast-skipping doesn't really help the dieter because he usually makes up for the missed meal later in the day. Nutritionally, it's wiser to spread one's calories through the day than to save them all for a dinner splurge (the body does not work off as many calories during sleep as it does during daily activity). Thus, dieters who consume most of their calories at night may find that the pounds drop off more slowly than those who eat three, even four, *light* meals during the day.

A number of nutritional studies have been conducted on the subject of breakfast and invariably, persons who skip breakfast perform more poorly during the morning than those who eat good breakfasts. They become groggy by mid-morning, their efficiency falls off. School children who eat little or no breakfast are generally unable to concentrate on their studies *OR* upon games during morning recess.

The menus and recipes that follow prove that nutritious breakfasts can be appetizing without being overwhelming, that they can be made easily and efficiently even by "owls" who function best later in the day.

243

THE FAVORITE BREAKFAST FOODS:

CEREALS—SOME BASICS AND BUYING TIPS

Treasure Land of Variety

Take your pick—wheat, corn, rice, oats, barley—for all are waiting to win your favor. Cereals that cook fast enough to be called "instant" appeal to the hot-breakfast group. Youngsters, particularly, go for the ready-to-eat varieties. And even Baby has his breakfast tailored for him. All may eat their choice as biscuits, kernels, alphabets, animals, flakes, or puffs that have been popped, shredded, or rolled into many shapes; presweetened with sugar or honey; flavored with cocoa or fruit; mixed with freeze-dry fruits; or ready-prepared from a jar.

Budget Bell Ringers

All cereals are good buys, for they give so much for so little. The kinds to be cooked, especially whole-grain ones, are the thriftiest. For example, one ounce of rolled oats cooks into a two-thirds-cup serving of oatmeal for an average of just 1½¢. Ready-to-eat cereals naturally cost more per serving, for all the fixing has been done for you. And single-serving packs, plus the new presweetened and low-calorie cereals are still higher. Two good guides for buying are: When pennies count the most, you spend wisely on whole-grain or enriched cereals that take cooking. When you want variety or convenience, have the fun of trying the many different ready-to-eat cereals.

Big Packages vs. Little Ones

Not only is there little difference, if any, between the cost per ounce of a small and an economy-size box, but cereal prices stay about the same the year round. If your family is small, stick to the smaller sizes so you can buy oftener and in greater variety. If your family is large and a cereal-loving one, your better buys are the giant-size packages. And don't be influenced by the size and shape of the box. Instead, compare price with weight, then figure the cost you are paying per ounce. Today you'll find squatty packages (containing the same weight as tall ones) and you may find they store more easily without tipping or spilling.

At Home, Store Cereals This Way

A cool dry shelf in the kitchen is your best and handiest storage spot, and the package the cereal comes in is its best keeper, for each manufacturer has worked hard to bring you his product in its freshest state. Read label directions for opening all packages. Some have a pull-out thread that unseals the cover quickly and neatly, making it easy to recap for storing. Others have a pour spout or an inner waxed bag with plenty of fold-over. These conveniences are designed to help you keep cereals crisp and fresh to the last serving in the box.

In Cooking, Use Cereals These Ways

Follow our grandmothers' way with thrifty farina and corn meal for breading chops, cutlets, fish, croquettes, and chicken. Along with the up-to-the-minute packaged cornflake crumbs, these cereals are still No. 1 favorites for these cooking jobs.

Use cereals as a stretcher or to add extra flavor and nourishment these ways: Stir farina or crushed bite-size wheat biscuits into meatloaf mixture, rolled oats or crisp rice flakes into cooky batter; or try corn flakes or fruit-flavor or sugared cereals as toppings for fruit Betty.

Save any bits of dry cereals in a jar, then crush or whirl in a blender for a ready-to-use crumb topper for baked dishes or scalloped vegetables.

In Serving, Try These Flavor Tips

Mix two ready-to-eat cereals of different shapes and flavors—oven-toasted rice with whole-wheat shreds, corn flakes with puffed wheat, wheat flakes with bite-size rice biscuits, whole bran with crisp oat cereal.

Vary the milk. Skim milk, of course, is a dieter's friend. And children, especially, love chocolate milk or malted milk poured over their cereal. Beat preserves or a mild spice such as nutmeg or cinnamon into plain milk. Add a "drink-an-egg" to milk by beating one into a cup of sweetened milk, as for eggnog.

Use breakfast juice—orange, fruit nectar, or prune—in place of milk.

Change the sweetener. Brown sugar, 10X (confectioners' powdered) sugar, cinnamon-sugar, honey, maple syrup, molasses, chocolate syrup, jam, and jelly are just a few choices for variety. And for calorie counters, there are both no-calorie sweeteners and diet-sweetened cereals.

A QUICK *Q AND A* ON CEREALS

Q. *Why are some cereal packages not quite full?*

A. Cereals are sold by weight, not volume, and the weight on the package is guaranteed. In the factory, each box is packed as full as practical. In shipping, the cereal is likely to settle a bit. If you question the quantity, try this experiment: Empty the box, then carefully spoon the cereal back in and see how much fuller the box is.

Q. *Can I eat all cereals if I am on a calorie-trimming diet?*

A. Yes, as a rule of thumb. An average serving of cereal is only about 100 calories, and, of course, it should be eaten with skim milk, which adds just 45 calories for each ½ cup. More good news for dieters are the low-calorie cereals that cut the count for each serving to between 60 and 75 calories for each 1 cup.

Q. *My recipes sometimes call for "wheat germ"? What is it?*

A. Wheat germ is the heart of the wheat grain that is removed in processing. It looks like a fine golden flake, has a nutlike flavor, and is a rich source of protein, vitamins, and minerals. Look for it in jars, and use just as is to sprinkle over hot or cold cereal or mix into special recipes such as meat loaf and cookies.

Q. *Why are some rolled oats marked quick-cooking? May I use them the same as regular rolled oats in a recipe since I seldom have both kinds on hand?*

A. The difference between regular or old-fashioned and quick-cooking or instant rolled oats is this: Regular is made by rolling each steam-softened oat kernel into one large flake. Quick-cooking is simply this same large flake cut into three pieces before rolling. The smaller and thinner the flake, the quicker the cooking. It's that simple. In cooking, unless your recipe specifically calls for regular or instant rolled oats, you may use either with equally good results.

SOME WAYS TO SIMPLIFY BREAKFAST-MAKING

Spend a few minutes at night thinking about tomorrow's breakfast and see what a good

morning it brings to everyone. These plan-aheads from freezer, refrigerator, and cupboard work almost like magic.

Freezer Make-Aheads

Make French toast, following your favorite recipe, then cool, wrap, and freeze it. In the morning, take out what you need and pop it into the toaster to heat—no thawing needed. (Remember this heat-and-eat way with pancakes and waffles too—either homemade or the store-bought frozen kind.) Spread with big spoonfuls of cottage cheese and jam or hot butter-blended syrup.

• Have fruit juice ready in a shake with this jiffy trick: The night before, place frozen concentrate just as it comes from the can in a container with tight-fitting lid; measure in water; chill. In the morning, simply shake.

• Save bits of bacon or ham left from another meal to stir into scrambled eggs or omelets. Crumble or dice them, if needed; bundle into foil packets and freeze. At breakfast time, meat's ready without the fuss of cooking.

Refrigerator Timesavers

Mix eggs to scramble in top of double boiler; chill overnight. In the morning, set over hot water and cook—little watching needed.

Stir up pancake batter the night before and chill. When ready to bake, thin with a little milk.

Plan breakfast, Dutch style, with ready-to-serve meat and cheese to eat with buttery hot toast. A slice or two of beef, lamb, veal, or pork from a dinner roast or sandwich cold cuts, along with one or two kinds of cheese, make an appetizing and satisfying plate—different, too.

Flavor butter or margarine with maple syrup, frozen concentrated orange or grape juice, or spice lightly with nutmeg, cinnamon, or cardamom to keep on hand for pancakes or toast.

Spread toast with peanut butter, soft cheese spread, or cottage cheese for a flavor change.

Cupboard-Shelf Helpers

Heat canned applesauce; spoon on hot buttered toast; sprinkle with cinnamon-sugar.

Slice or dice shelled hard-cooked eggs and stir into hot cream sauce made "instantly" with canned cream of mushroom, celery, or chicken soup. Spoon over toast or toasted English muffins.

245

BREAKFAST

Spread hot buttered toast generously with canned deviled ham, top with fried, poached, or scrambled eggs.

Stir a few raisins or chopped dried prunes or apricots into hot cooked cereal, or top each bowlful with drained canned peaches, apricots, pears, or plums for a fruit-and-cereal course all in one.

Fix packaged precooked rice to serve with milk or cream, a dollop of butter or margarine, or a sprinkling of cinnamon, nutmeg, or cinnamon-sugar.

SOME UNBORING BREAKFASTS

Four Lazy-Day Breakfasts:

When breakfast is a daily family-round-the-table meal, for lazy weekends—or whenever there's time to dawdle—plan one of the following four breakfasts. (Recipes are included for those dishes starred in menus.)

*Orange Peaks
or
Grapefruit-Pineapple Juice
Dry Cereal
Milk
*Skillet Scramble with Slivered Ham
Raisin Toast
Corn Muffins
Jam
Marmalade
Coffee
Milk

Orange Peaks

For each serving, halve a seedless orange from stem to blossom end, then cut each half into four wedges; halve wedges crosswise to make 16 peaked chunks. This is finger food—each piece is bite-size. Children love them.

246

Skillet Scramble with Slivered Ham
Makes 4 servings

6 eggs
⅓ cup milk
½ teaspoon salt
⅛ teaspoon pepper
2 tablespoons butter or margarine
1 package (1 ounce) Gruyère cheese, cut in small cubes
1 cup matchstick slivers of cooked ham (or bologna)

1 Beat eggs until frothy with milk, salt and pepper.

2 Melt butter or margarine in a medium-size frying pan (do not let it bubble); pour in egg mixture; lower heat; cook slowly. As eggs begin to thicken, stir from the bottom with a wide rubber spatula or pancake turner to keep them in large creamy puffs.
3 Fold Gruyère cheese into eggs while they are still moist; remove from heat (eggs continue to cook from their own heat and cheese melts quickly).
4 Spoon onto a heated serving dish and garnish with matchstick slivers of ham.

*California Compote
*Baked Banana-Sausage Sticks
*Sally Lunn Muffin Squares
Jam
Butter
Coffee
Milk

California Compote
Makes 4 servings

1 package (1 pound) dried prunes
2 cups reconstituted frozen pineapple-orange juice

1 Place dried prunes in a 6-cup baking dish; cover with pineapple-orange juice; cover and let stand overnight at room temperature.
2 While preheating oven for Baked Banana-sausage Sticks and Sally Lunn Muffin Squares (recipes follow), slide dish of prunes into oven and let warm 5 to 10 minutes. Serve warm.

Baked Banana-Sausage Sticks
Bake at 400° for 15 minutes. Makes 4 servings

1 package (8 ounces) heat-and-serve sausages
2 bananas
1 tablespoon lemon juice
4 tablespoons brown sugar

1 Arrange sausages in single layer in shallow baking pan, 9x13x2; halve bananas; cut halves lengthwise in two; arrange, cut side up, in single

Baked bananas aren't the usual breakfast fruit, but they make a very welcome change of pace—and taste.